A
WINE
Miscellany

A
WINE
Miscellany

GRAHAM HARDING

MICHAEL O'MARA BOOKS LIMITED

First published in Great Britain in 2005 by
Michael O'Mara Books Limited
9 Lion Yard, Tremadoc Road
London sw4 7nq

A CIP catalogue record for this book is available
from the British Library

ISBN 1-84317-176-6

1 3 5 7 9 10 8 6 4 2

www.mombooks.com

Designed and typeset by Martin Bristow

Printed and bound in Finland by WS Bookwell, Juva

Introduction

WINE IS NOT JUST 'the fermented juice of grapes', to quote the European Commission's less than poetic definition.

Rituals surround it, high-paid lawyers battle over it, huge sums of money are made and lost buying and selling it.

It's better for your health than almost any other substance – but only if you stick to two glasses a day.

It's an instrument of seduction, an expression of personality. It's a world.

This book is about that hidden world of wine.

So far as I can verify, it is (or was at the time of writing) all true, except for the obvious and uncheckable myths. However, mistakes undoubtedly remain. For these I apologize.

Enjoy it, but remember that not everything in this book can be safely tried at home.

I owe thanks to many people who knowingly or unknowingly inspired this book. My father started buying first-growth clarets in

the 1950s (on an annual budget of £50). I greatly benefited. Michael Palij MW and Charles Garrett were inspirational teachers in their Oxford-based wine courses. My colleagues in those courses and in the Oxford Wine Club remain friends and wine companions. Lastly, my wife Kay. Without her present of the initial Wine Matters course and her subsequent toleration of my frequent wine-related absences, this book could not have been written. But she claims to have enjoyed the wine education by proxy.

GRAHAM HARDING
Oxford, 2005

VINTAGE VINTAGES

The earliest fermented beverage of which there is archaeological evidence dates back around 9,000 years. Chinese pottery shards from 7,000 BC show evidence of a mixed fermented drink made from either hawthorn or grapes. The next oldest wine – almost certainly grape-based – was traced from pottery found in the Neolithic complex at Hajji Firuz Tepe in Iran.

There is little need to seek the origins of wine. Any grapes crushed in a rock hollow or left in a skin bag or pottery bowl in the heat of the summer will ferment. The Neolithic peoples would undoubtedly have noticed how the sweetness of the grapes was transformed into a liquid with different and intriguing properties.

A romantic Iranian legend speaks of a young lady intent on suicide after rejection by the king. Her chosen method was to drink the liquid residue of spoiled table grapes. She passed out but awoke to find that life was worth living after all – and was restored to the harem after passing on her discovery.

THE ORIGINS OF WINE

Wine of a different type – and very different vintage – was reportedly discovered by Chinese archaeologists in one of the tombs of the Western Han dynasty (206 BC to AD 25), in the city of Xi'an.

The rice wine had been stored in a bronze vessel with a raw lacquer seal that had kept it entirely airtight. The wine was described as having a light flavour and low alcohol content. It was, however, green. This may have been the result of oxidation from the bronze container, but Chinese wine experts say that some rice wine was fermented green.

Patrick McGovern is an American archaeologist who discovered the oldest traces of wine on pottery vessels dating back to 7,000 BC. He has also analysed a 3,000-year-old wine found hermetically sealed into bronze vessels. This wine had a floral odour on opening, though this dispersed almost immediately, and had been flavoured with herbs and flowers and – in one instance – with wormwood (the essence of absinthe).

WINE – BUT NOT AS WE KNOW IT

Wine is defined by the European Commission as the 'fermented juice of grapes'. As the notes above on ancient Chinese rice wine record, this definition excludes many types of wine. A recent addition to the pantheon of world 'wine' is Chinese fish wine. The wine, for which the official Chinese news agency Xinhua claims orders have already been received from a number of neighbouring countries, is said to be 'nutritious and contain low alcohol'.

In 2001, the Orkney Wine Company was established in Scotland after getting grants from the local council and the Highland Fund. The plan was to make wine with fruit and vegetables; a whisky and carrot blend was the first planned for commercial consumption. Turnip experiments were successful but it was felt the ingredients were unlikely to attract customers.

MARIJUANA WINE

Attractive (to some) but illegal in many jurisdictions is the following 'wine'.

This 'weedwine' recipe is from a US website (www.totse.com).

Ingredients

2 gal. boiling water
4–8 oz of fresh marijuana
5 lbs of sugar or 8 lbs of honey

3 oranges, sliced
3 lemons, sliced
2 cakes of yeast

Preparation

Place the fresh cannabis in the boiling water, and add the sugar, orange and lemon slices. Remove from heat and let stand for several days. Add yeast after straining into a clean container. Ferment for four weeks before racking and corking.

The ancients might (or might not) have approved of such a recipe. We do not know for certain how important grapes (as distinct from other fruits and vegetables) were, other than as the most easily fermented source of an intoxicating liquid. What is certain is that techniques of fermenting grapes were well advanced thousands of years ago and that wine had already become a business.

Pemberton's French Wine Coca

Coca wine, with cocaine, was already a flourishing market in late nineteenth-century America when Dr John S. Pemberton created his 'French Wine Coca' in 1886. He was a latecomer to the market, which was dominated by Angelo Mariani's Coca Wine. This product, conceived and marketed by a French priest, added cocaine to wine. Pemberton added both kola nuts and damiana (a natural aphrodisiac) to his drink and marketed it as an aid to overcoming morphine addiction. It was advertised as an 'intellectual beverage' with the capacity to 'invigorate the brain'. Cocaine was removed from the drink in 1904, though the Coca-Cola Company continued to use 'decocainised' coca leaves as flavouring for some decades. It is possible that they may still do so. In 2002, the Bolivian authorities authorised the export of 159 tonnes of coca leaf to the USA 'for the manufacturing of the soft drink, Coca-Cola'. The company was equivocal in its response to enquiries. 'The formula for Coca-Cola is a very closely guarded trade secret. Therefore we do not discuss the formula.' Make of that what you will.

The Commercial History

Five thousand years ago the Egyptians were confidently in control of the technology of winemaking, and wine had become a well-regulated commercial industry with distribution of casks by river and a code of conduct for wine-sellers.

The laws of Hammurabi, the sixth King of Babylon, make it clear that wine-sellers were women. This does not appear to have been a menial occupation. The Fourth Dynasty of Kish was founded in Sumer around 3,000 years BC by a woman who had been a wine-seller in her youth. The eternally seditious nature of bars and cafés is suggested by the king's ruling that if outlaws should hatch a conspiracy in the house of a wine-seller and she did not inform on them to the authorities then she herself should be put to death.

The Spread of Wine

Region	Time of arrival
China	7,000 BC
Mesopotamia	6,000 BC
Egypt	5,000 BC
Phoenicia (North Africa)	3,000 BC
Cyprus	3,000 BC
Greece and Crete	2,000 BC (earliest evidence is a stone footpress at a Minoan villa dated to 1,600 BC)
Southern/Central Europe	1,000–500 BC
Northern Europe (via the Roman Empire)	500 BC to AD 300

The Wine of Omar Khayyám

Writing around nine hundred years ago in his collection of poems, the *Rubáiyát*, the Persian poet Omar Khayyám sings the praises (at least in Edward Fitzgerald's translation) of 'a Jug of Wine, a Loaf of Bread – and Thou Beside me singing in the Wilderness.'

Which wine was he drinking? It was more likely to have been white than red, and more likely sweet than dry. It may well have come from the villages around Shiraz, an eighth-century town that legend says gave its name to the red wine grape we know as Syrah (Old World), or Shiraz (New World).

CHAMPAGNE OMAR

Omar's name has been borrowed by the Mumbai (previously Bombay) concern Château Indage for India's best-known (and best) 'champagne', a Chardonnay-based wine. Omar Khayyám is a dry and fragrant sparkling wine, and has a more alcoholic sister labelled Marquise de Pompadour. Though the 'Champagne India' name annoys the Champenois, it does have Piper-Heidsieck expertise behind it.

The Indians are becoming increasingly enthusiastic about wine and their consumption is growing at 20 per cent a year – albeit from a tiny base. There are around 200 million middle-class Indians who could potentially be turned on to wine. India is the world's second-largest producer of table grapes (after Chile), and Indian wines from the Sula vineyard in Maharashtra, west India, are now sold in Italy, France and the USA.

By Omar's time (*c.*1120 AD) certainly one and possibly two wine businesses still extant were in operation.

OLDEST WINE FAMILIES

Although the wine business was undoubtedly commercialized thousands of years ago, the oldest wine business still in existence goes back only a thousand years or so.

The oldest known wine business (almost certainly the oldest French business in any sector) is probably the Château de Goulaine, inhabited by the family of that name continuously since around the year 1,000. Its interests include wine production from the castle vineyards; however, it is not clear when wine was first produced for sale, rather than for family consumption. The company is reputed to be the third-oldest commercial concern in the world – after two Japanese businesses (one of which, a temple maker, dates back to AD 578).

The Ricasoli family interests in wine and olive oil in Italy go back to at least 1141, when the Republic of Florence gifted them land near Siena. Bettino Ricasoli is credited with having created the original recipe for Chianti by combining two red grapes, Sangiovese and Canaiolo, with two white grapes, Malvasia and Trebbiano. It is the fourth-oldest family business in the world.

The Antinori family concern of Florence, the ninth oldest wine business, traces its involvement in wine back to Giovanni di Piero Antinori's acceptance into the Florentine Guild of Vintners in 1385. The current Piero Antinori and his three daughters still run a wine empire that stretches from Italy to the Americas and takes in Malta, Hungary and Chile.

Back in France, the Coussergues family has produced wine since 1495 and is now into the sixteenth generation of the family. It is the eleventh oldest wine family.

The Codorníu estate in Spain, like the Fonjallaz business in Switzerland, dates back to the mid-sixteenth century. The third-oldest French business, that of the Hugel family in Alsace, dates back to 1639 when the family started to make wine in Riquewihr, though its roots go back to at least the fifteenth century. Wine merchants do not enter the lists until the seventeenth century.

OLDEST WINE MERCHANTS

By common consent the world's oldest active wine merchant is Berry Bros & Rudd – still operating from 3 St James's Street in London. The shop here was opened by the Widow Bourne in 1698. George Berry did not take over the business until 1803, by which date the firm had been supplying the British royal family with wine for over forty years. Non-wine note: Cutty Sark whisky (America's best selling whisky of the 1960s and 1970s) was created at 3 St James's Street in 1923.

Hedges & Butler, another UK company, claims to have been founded in 1667 but is no longer independent and trades merely as a retail brand within the Bass business. Its distinguished whisky brands are now owned by Ian Macleod and Co. Ltd, an independent Scottish distillery. Macleod and Co. are (or were) also responsible for the 'tonic wine', Wincarnis. This is a blend of wine and meat (*vin* plus *carnis*) which was also known as Liebig's Extract of Meat and Malt Wine. Enough said.

The oldest American merchant is Acker Merrall & Condit. The company was formed in 1820 and carries a range of wines priced from $4 to $19,000 (£2.50 to £11,000). The company is now the pre-eminent American wine auctioneer on the East Coast.

CHAUCER'S WINE

Though his father's wine-importing business has not survived, the fourteenth-century English poet Geoffrey Chaucer reflected in his poems an upbringing surrounded by wine and food.

Chaucer was the son of a wealthy wine importer. Born around 1340, he had parallel careers as an official of the royal court and as a poet. His work as customs officer, forester and royal clerk rewarded him not just with salaries and annuities but also with daily pitchers of wine and, later on in his life, a yearly barrel of wine. His courtly poems make little mention of food and wine and James Matterer, an expert on Chaucerian cookery, believes Chaucer was not greatly consumed by passions for food and wine. However, his late master-piece, *The Canterbury Tales*, which focuses on the emerging middle classes of fourteenth-century England, uses food and wine to illustrate the character of each of the pilgrims whose tales he tells.

'The Summoner's Tale' in particular gives graphic accounts of the way in which alcohol and intoxication fuel a tyrant's taste for

brutality. Despite warnings from a courtier that 'wine causes man to lose, and wretchedly, his mind, and his limbs' usages', Cambyses, a king who enjoys his drink, kills the courtier's son with an arrow to demonstrate that his 'might of hand and foot' and his eyesight are unimpaired by the effects of wine.

In other tales, wine has a gentler role. Chaucer has his characters talk of 'ypocras', 'vernage' and 'clarree'. Vernage was a sweet Italian wine. The name lives on as Vernaccia. Both ypocras and clarree were, in effect, mulled wines, sweetened and spiced to act as aperitifs and/or digestifs.

Medieval Wines

Ypocras – named after the Greek physician Hippocrates – was an after-dinner digestif. It would be made with either red or white wine but the former was usually preferred since its robustness was held to promote good digestion. A modern recipe for ypocras calls for a bottle of inexpensive red wine (preferably sweet) that is brought to the boil with 30 cl. of honey (or 300 g of sugar). Add more honey or sugar to ensure it is appropriately sweet for your taste. Skim off any scum from the top of the liquid, allow it to cool and add a tablespoon of each of the following spices: ginger, cinnamon, cardamom, white pepper, clove, nutmeg and caraway seed. Stand the liquid in a cool place for twenty-four hours, then strain through several layers of cheesecloth (or coffee filters). Repeat if necessary for maximum clarity. Mature for a month at least.

Clarree was also flavoured with honey and spices. Usually made with sweet white wine, it too should be boiled first with honey. The spice mix is less extensive: one tablespoon each of cinnamon, ginger and cardamom and a teaspoon of white pepper. As with ypocras, clarree should be strained and matured. The name comes from *vinum claratum*, or clarified wine, and is said to be the ancestor of the term 'claret'.

Both these recipes come – in adapted form – from *The Forme of Curye* (c.1390), compiled by and for cooks in the household of Richard II.

Served chilled, clarree is recommended as an aperitif. Ypocras would be taken at the end of the meal or possibly with a final late-night snack called the *voide*, which featured sweet fruits, cakes and spiced wine as a nightcap.

Sir John and His Wines

Another drinker whose name, and those of his preferred drinks, has survived the centuries is Shakespeare's lecherous knight Sir John Falstaff.

'A good sherris-sack hath a two-fold operation in it,' says Sir John in *Henry IV, Part 2*, Act IV. Sack was Sir John's tipple. Sherris (i.e. Jerez) was simply the place of production. It was not a fortified wine and was probably around 16 per cent alcohol. In London it would have been sweetened – perhaps at Falstaff's London base, the Boar's Head Tavern in Eastcheap. Occasionally the wine was adulterated (in Falstaff's view) by the addition of 'pullet-sperm', or beaten eggs.

The name 'sack' comes from the Spanish word *sacar* meaning 'to take out' or 'export'. It was primarily an export wine. The Spanish, despite their uneasy relations with England, made the wine for English tastes and around two-thirds of the annual production of 60,000 butts (casks) went to England and the Netherlands. It is possible that the wine that Shakespeare was thinking of had come from one of Sir Francis Drake's more famous exploits. In 1587, Drake sailed into the harbour at Cádiz, where the Armada fleet was preparing for sea, and sacked and burned thirty-two ships. Among his trophies were 2,900 butts of sack that were ready for loading. The wine came home with him and was sold as part of the spoils.

A hundred and fifty years or so after the fictional Sir John was imbibing by the pint and praising sack's ability to make his brain 'apprehensive, forgetive, full of nimble, fiery and delectable shapes', the name had shifted to sherry. Sack survives only in Shakespeare and in the Dry Sack brand of sherry that thrives in the UK and USA.

OLDEST VINES

Producers, merchants and their wines far outlast the humble vines.

The phylloxera louse that devastated the late nineteenth-century European wine industry means that claims for the world's oldest vines from anywhere except Australia are rather dubious. The only pre-phylloxera vines that survive in Europe were those planted in sandy soil. The best examples are Bollinger's Vieilles Vignes in the Champagne region and the remarkable survival of the Ramisco wines grown in trenches on the sand dunes outside Lisbon.

SLOVENIAN SURVIVOR

There is a single vine in the Slovenian city of Maribor that is accepted as the oldest in the world. It is more than four-hundred-years old and produces between 35 and 55 kilograms of Ametovka grapes per year. The hundred or so 25 cl. bottles produced from these grapes are mainly reserved for ceremonial gifts. Some are sold to collectors. The wine is described as sweet and rich – not surprising, given that Ametovka is primarily a table grape.

Aussie Oldies

There are reports of Traminer vines dating from the 1750s or there-abouts in Rhodt, southern Germany, but the oldest authenticated vines are probably those of the Turkey Flat Vineyards in Australia. Pioneer settler Johann Fiedler planted Shiraz vines on the bank of the Tanunda Creek in the Barossa Valley in 1847. The renowned American wine writer Robert Parker gave the 2002 Shiraz 94 points (out of a theoretical maximum of 100) and raved about its 'glorious fruit with notes of crème de cassis, raspberry liqueur and liquorice'.

Hewitson's 'Old Garden' Mourvèdre is made from vines planted in the Barossa Valley in 1853. The wine is commercially available and earns ecstatic tasting notes praising its concentration, powerful sweet-cherry and dark-berry fruit and great balance of acidity and peppery tannins. Château Tahbilk's Old Vine Shiraz is produced from ungrafted pre-phylloxera vines planted in 1869. A recent tasting note on the 1860 Vines Shiraz refers to its 'mature stewed berries', its length, and its earthy, leathery notes on the nose.

Les Vieilles Vignes de France

Bollinger's Vieilles Vignes are 100 per cent Pinot Noir. A few plots in Aÿ and Bouzy resisted the phylloxera louse and are now cultivated manually with traditional tools. In good years (only thirty-three vintages since 1921) a Vieilles Vignes champagne is made, and typically costs $400 (£230) per bottle. It is unclear exactly how old the vines are and another French candidate for the oldest vines may be those of Domaine Lafond. These were planted in 1880, just after the phylloxera attack, in what is now the heart of the Côtes du Rhône appellation.

THE GRANDFATHER

America's oldest Zinfandel vineyard is probably the Grandpère vineyard in Amador County, California, which was planted in the 1850s (though its initial production was mainly table grapes). Some experts believe that vineyards planted with Mission grapes still survive from the days when the grape was used for communion wine.

MILLENNIAL *TERROIR*

Wines far outlive the vines that produce them, though the impact of *terroir* (that mystical combination of soil, climate and topography) is longer-lasting yet. The Clos Vougeot in Burgundy was first identified and pieced together by monks in the eleventh century and, though now much fragmented by the Napoleonic law of succession, it still produces wine of ethereal beauty. The ground is so valuable that it is said that the vineyard workers' boots are 'harvested' at the end of each shift to recover the soil. After heavy rains the growers are reputed to take shovels to the run-offs – again to recover the soil. It was also said that when, in the nineteenth century, a French regiment marched past the property it was the custom for it to halt and present arms.

THE OLDEST WINE

Hugh Johnson, in his magisterial *The Story of Wine*, describes a tasting in 1961 of a 1540 wine. This was a Steinwein, from the vineyard near Würzburg that looks down on the River Rhine. The year 1540 was extraordinarily hot and the wine had survived as a 'living organism' (as Johnson puts it). It had lived in a grand cask for most of its life, topped up as required with wine of an equivalent quality, but was bottled some two hundred years after vinification. Johnson describes it as a 'brown, Madeira-like fluid' that 'hinted of its German origins'. However, the topping-up process may undermine this Steinwein's claim to be the oldest ever tasted.

CROMWELLIAN TOKAY

James Halliday, Australian winemaker and connoisseur, describes a bottle of 1646 Tokay he shared with wine expert and bon viveur Len Evans in the 1970s. This was at the first meeting of the Single Bottle Club in Australia (see page 169). Halliday recorded his impressions of the wine as 'dried out but still very sound'. The lack of a more detailed note is explained by the later admission that he had forgotten where he filed the notes of this particular dinner. Given that 'Cromwell was stalking the fields in England when this was made,' the Club was not unsatisfied with the wine's flavour. A bottle of the same 1646 vintage was sold in 1984 in Geneva for $700 (£400) to John A. Chunko of Princeton, New Jersey. This may be the oldest Tokay anyone living will ever taste. At the beginning of the Second World War the cellar of the merchant house of Fukier in Warsaw contained 328 bottles of 1606 Tokay. At the end of the war there was none. Russian troops had taken their pick and drunk their fill. Not a single bottle has subsequently surfaced.

THE WINE OF POMPEII

We don't know what Roman wine tasted like but we do know that the inhabitants of the city of Pompeii, which was buried in the volcanic eruption of AD 79, enjoyed the results. Frescoes of drinkers are to be found in Pompeii and there were dozens of bars and willing girls to serve the wine. Vineyards within the city walls are preserved with their cellars and terracotta storage jars, or *doli*.

In all, evidence of five vineyards was discovered in Pompeii, and one has been re-created. It is the work of a partnership between the Archaeological Superintendent of Pompeii and the Mastroberardino family of winemakers, who have worked to preserve Campania's viticultural heritage.

THE BERARDINO EFFECT

Had it not been for Antonio Mastroberardino, it is probable that the vines brought to Italy by the ancient Greeks, vines such as Aglianico, Greco di Tufo and Fiano d'Avellino, would have died out after the Second World War.

Mastroberardino was head of the tenth generation of a famous winemaking family and his son, Piero, heads the Villa dei Misteri project that has re-created the wine of 2,000 years ago. Pompeiian frescoes and descriptions in the viticultural (grape-cultivating) writings of Pliny and Columella (an agrarian writer of the first century AD whose *De Re Rustica* is the most detailed study of ancient winemaking we have) enabled the precise vines to be identified and replanted. Piedirosso and Sciascinoso (or Olivella) showed the most promise and were planted at the Pompeiian density of 8,000 vines per hectare. They were trained on chestnut stakes planted in the holes left by the original stakes 2,000 years ago.

DEAD MICE AND OPEN *DOLI*

The Villa dei Misteri project has preserved ancient methods of training, pruning and harvesting, although not every Roman practice has been followed. The Romans would have fermented their wine in open *doli* (earthenware jars) buried to their necks in the earth to cool the fermenting must (the unfermented or fermenting juice of grapes). Piero Mastroberardino has chosen long maceration (the term for keeping the grapes in contact with the fermenting liquid), long wood ageing (the Roman historian, Pliny, recommended ten years) and bottling unfiltered wine.

In his writings on viticulture, Pliny also recommends burning the corpses of any mice that drown in the *doli* and then tipping the ashes back into the mixture. This tradition is now frowned upon. Nor today is the wine stored in resinated amphorae (tall, narrow clay vessels) since this practice kills aroma and adds an intense pine taste. This would have been less important to the Romans, whose wine was typically spiced up with herbs and sweeteners as well as being watered down from its alcohol levels of 20 per cent or more.

The modern product – named Villa dei Misteri – is a concentrated, almost opaque red wine with red-fruit aromas and hints of pepper and spice. Initial comments were varied. Some said 'soft and spicy'; others that the wine was over-tannic, and that more time was needed for maturation.

Only 1,721 bottles were made from the 2001 harvest and many of these were retained for further maturation (though some were auctioned off to raise funds for further restoration).

'THE ABSENCE OF DEFECTS IS NOT THE PRESENCE OF VIRTUES'

Sean Thackrey is a Californian winemaker who has gone medieval. His wines are made according to the precepts of ancient texts, not twentieth-century science. He lets the grapes 'rest' outside for twenty-four hours before fermenting the juice in open-top vats under the eucalyptus trees on his land. Resting the grape allows microbes to bloom on the surface of the damaged fruit. These 'defects' make for a wider range of flavours. Despite his laid-back and instinctive approach to winemaking his top wines score high Parker points. His Petite Sirah rates 96 Parker points and his Orion wine (labelled as 'California Native Red Wine') 94 points. He also claims that his wines taste better the day after they are opened – contrary to received wisdom.

MADEIRA, M'DEAR?

A 'quite drinkable' seventeenth-century Madeira was claimed at the time to be 'the oldest wine that anyone now living has tasted'. Two bottles laid up by an artillery officer in the cellar of his house in Spitalfields, London, in the 1670s were discovered in 1999 by archaeologists working for the Museum of London. The cork on one had perished but the other was still intact. A small sample of wine was tasted by – among others – Michael Broadbent MW, arguably the world's greatest authority on historic vintages (see page 113), and David Molyneux-Berry, Head of Wine at Sotheby's. The experts were divided in their assessment but both agreed that it was drinkable, though 'fresh' and very dry (a positive assessment) or 'a bit sharp' (somewhat less positive).

Madeira is known to be virtually indestructible. Thanks to the heat treatment the wines are subjected to, an open bottle will keep for months or years without spoiling. Very often the wine is stored upright, as in some of the earliest American cellars. Savannah in Georgia, in particular, is famous for its ancient Madeiras, whose labels record not only the names of the ships that brought them to the East Coast of America, but also the names of those who have owned the wine.

Undersea Madeira

Another seventeenth-century Madeira, tasted in 2000, came from a Dutch warship sunk in the Wadden Sea. The bottle, which was green and gourd-shaped, was probably the property of a Dutch naval officer. The tasting notes from Lucette Faber, a Dutch wine historian, speak of 'old marmalade and nuts'. She also detected the taste and hue of elderberry juice – an ingredient of wines of the Douro, Portugal, at the time (and at least into the late nineteenth century). Chemical analysis indicated high levels of acidity in the wine, which could have been caused by the addition of the elderberry juice.

Vin Jaune – Age and Oxidation

Another exceptionally long-living wine is Vin Jaune, from the Château Chalon region of France. In November 1994 a bottle that had won a gold medal at the Paris Exhibition of 1868 was re-tasted. The wine, dating from 1774, was described as clear and bright with an intense, fine bouquet, well-bodied, with noticeable wood influence and an exceptionally long finish. The owner still has a few bottles left.

Vin Jaune owes its longevity to a deliberate oxidation process. The wine, made from Savagnin grapes in the Jura, is vinified as normal and then left to mature in old barrels with a large surface area exposed. On this surface a *voile*, or veil, of yeast develops in a similar fashion to the *flor* on a sherry cask. The wine is left in the barrels for six years and three months before bottling in 62 cl. clavelin bottles.

Local producers claim this size represents what is left of a litre of wine after the completion of the lengthy process. The taste is nutty and intense.

THE OLDEST AUSTRALIAN WINE

The oldest Australian wine is believed to be a bottle of 1867 Tintara Vineyards Association Claret, purchased at Sotheby's in 1977 and now owned by B. R. L. Hardy, the Australian wine giant that is part of Constellation Brands. Even if the office cleaner's duster had not knocked over a bottle of 1864 Gilbert Pewsey Vale Cabernet that Australian wineman extraordinaire Len Evans had bought, it is likely that the Tintara would still remain the oldest bottle of Australian wine. Evans planned to make the 1864 wine the centrepiece of one of his Single Bottle Club dinners.

All these wines – bar the 1540 Steinwein mentioned earlier – come (or came) in a bottle. Without the bottle and the ability to store wines that it confers we would have no fine-wine industry.

JUGS AND BOTTLES

Wine was served for centuries from pottery and, later, pewter jugs. It was drawn direct from the barrel and brought to the table. The problem with opaque containers is that it is difficult to spot when

the sediment from unfiltered wine is about to spoil the drinker's enjoyment.

In the seventeenth century, bottles started to be used for serving wine, though not for storing it. Bottles would be taken to a wine merchant for filling – as the great diarist Samuel Pepys did in 1663 when his diary records that he went to the Mitre to see his wine put into his 'crested bottles'. Crested bottles were those marked with the owner's seal on the shoulder, and such bottles would be treasured and reused.

Most seventeenth-century bottles were of a form known as 'shaft and globe' after their spherical bodies and long straight necks. The shape made them unsuitable for 'binning' on their sides for storage, and only in the 1720s did flatter-sided bottles enter common usage and enable the development of the wine cellar as we know it today – with, ideally, hundreds or thousands of bottles stored on their sides.

RAVENSCROFT'S REVENGE

Crystal decanters – introduced to England in the 1670s after George Ravenscroft had discovered (or copied from the Venetians) the secret of lead crystal glass – enabled the drinker both to see when the sediment had settled to the bottom and when to stop pouring. The term 'decanter' itself was not in common usage for another fifty years or so following Ravenscroft's discovery, but it became de rigueur in the nineteenth century. In 1849, Lord Cardigan placed an officer on a charge for pouring direct from the bottle rather than from a decanter.

Bottles were, however, highly prized items in Britain until the middle of the nineteenth century, when the glass tax was repealed for the last time. This reduced both overall costs and the heavy bias against clear glass, which attracted tax eleven times greater than coloured. Around the beginning of the nineteenth century the French wine industry created the standard shapes we know today, when the first bottle-making machines replaced the glass-blowers. Of the two most common styles – the Bordeaux and the Burgundy bottles – the former is the more recent. Its more sharply angled shoulder is harder to blow by hand but far more effective in trapping sediment.

THE PUNTER'S TRICK

Dr Karl Blanks, a Cambridge University scientist, has developed a formula for estimating the price of a bottle by measuring the depth of the punt – the indentation at the foot of the bottle. Nobody now knows what the punt was actually for. The prime theory is that it helps to collect and hold the sediment thrown by older wines. Dr Blanks's discovery was that the deeper the dimple, the more expensive the bottle. His formula is expressed thus: take the dimple depth (in millimetres) and add 3.49. Divide the result by 4.3144. This will give you an estimate for the value of a red wine. For white wine, subtract £1.00. His website suggests that the results are only valid for wines costing between £5 and £10.

BOTTLE SIZES

Name	Bottle equivalent	Capacity
Split	Quarter bottle	18.7 cl.
Half bottle	Half bottle	37.5 cl.
Bottle	One bottle	75 cl.
Magnum	Two bottles	1.5 litres
Marie-Jeanne (champagne)	Three bottles	2.25 litres
Jeroboam (champagne and Burgundy)	Four bottles	3 litres
Double magnum (Burgundy and champagne)	Four bottles	3 litres
Jeroboam (Bordeaux)	Six bottles	4.5 litres
Rehoboam	Six bottles	4.5 litres
Impériale	Eight bottles	6 litres
Methuselah (Burgundy)	Eight bottles	6 litres
Salamanazar	Twelve bottles	9 litres
Balthazar (champagne)	Sixteen bottles	12 litres
Nebuchadnezzar (champagne)	Twenty bottles	15 litres

The 50 cl. bottle which is frequently encountered for port, Tokay and many sweet wines has no name.

In the early twentieth century, an American company produced oversized corkscrews for the larger bottles. However, now the necks of these bottles are manufactured to the same size as those of standard bottles, such corkscrews are no longer necessary.

IMPÉRIALE DESTRUCTION

A clerical error in 2002 (the shipper's, not excisemen's) led to HM Customs destroying an impériale of Château Mouton-Rothschild 1996 valued at £2,500, as well as cases of a range of other first-growths valued at £130,000. The wine was destroyed because of a lack of storage space.

THE WORLD'S LARGEST BOTTLE . . .

The world's largest bottle – a Maximus – stands 1.35 metres tall and weighs 153 kilograms (337 pounds). It cost a New Jersey wine and chocolate shop, which wanted it as a display centrepiece, almost $56,000 (£32,000) at a Sotheby's auction in 2004. The bottle, which was made by Czech glass-blowers, holds 173 bottles of 2001 Napa Valley Cabernet Sauvignon from Beringer Vineyards, which is approximately 1,350 glasses. Bought by the case, the wine would have cost around $2,000 (£1,150). The auction proceeds went to Share Our Strength, a famine charity.

. . . AND THE SMALLEST

The world's smallest bottles stand just under 3.5 centimetres tall. The hand-blown bottles contain 0.75 ml. of wine – almost all from fine vineyards. Guigal's Côte-Rôtie 'La Turque' costs $40 (£23); Clos Vougeot the same; Richebourg from Gros Frère et Soeur is $90 (£52), but it boasts a 24-carat gold seal. Each wine is limited to an edition of 1,000 bottles. Understandably, many are bought by collectors of doll's houses.

ULLAGE, SCHMULLAGE

'Ullage' is the technical term for the space between the cork and the wine. As wines age they often lose their liquid through evaporation. The level of the surface of the wine lowers from just below the cork to several centimetres lower. This level is important when buying wine at auction, and the catalogues will give a note of it. The lower the level, the greater the chance that the wine will have been spoiled.

BROADBENT'S DEFINITION OF ULLAGE

These generally accepted definitions come from Christie's wine catalogues and were first published in the late 1980s. Michael Broadbent MW is said to regret his failure to copyright the terms.

For Bordeaux wine, the fill level and their implications are given below.

Fill level	Ullage (cm)	Implication/comment
High fill	0.3	Normal level of young wines (and re-corked older wines).
Into neck	0.5	Acceptable at any age. Excellent in older wines.
Top shoulder	1.5	Normal for older wines (fifteen years plus).
Upper shoulder	2.5	Usually fine in older wines. Acceptable in wines over twenty years old.
Mid-shoulder	3.0	Buy at your own risk.
Mid-low shoulder	3.5	Greater risk. Price will reflect this.
Low shoulder	6.0	Definitely risky.
Below low shoulder	7.0	Often undrinkable. Buyer beware!

Burgundies are less susceptible to damage from low levels of fill. Below low shoulder, while seriously risky in old Bordeaux, is not usually a problem in pre-Second World War Burgundies. The condition of the cork is also a key factor in preserving old wines. If the wine has not been regularly re-corked then its quality will be threatened, which is why many top-grade châteaux have re-corking programmes.

Re-corking

Australian producer Penfolds runs Red Wine Re-corking Clinics. Described by the company as the 'ultimate in after-sales service', the clinics offer owners of Penfolds wines older than fifteen years the chance to have their wines checked out. If they pass the taste test administered by winemaker Peter Gago – dubbed 'Dr Death' by British wine writer Tim Atkin MW – then they are topped up, re-corked and recapsuled on the spot. In the twelve years they have been running the service Penfolds have re-corked around 50,000 bottles.

Stoppers

The question of stoppers has always been a vexed one. The first stoppers were probably made of pinewood. They were inserted into the necks of clay amphorae and sealed with a mix of resin and clay.

It was this mixture that gave the wines the flavour of resin, and contributed to the ancient world's love of the taste of retsina – the name for a wine, usually white, that is flavoured with resin. Before this time there were no stoppers – just a layer of oil on top of the wine to prevent insects and the air from spoiling the contents of the amphora.

Ground-glass stoppers were introduced in the sixteenth and seventeenth centuries. These superseded the waxed cloth and leather used until then and had the advantage of producing an airtight seal, provided that each was individually ground to fit the highly variable widths of bottlenecks available at the time. These stoppers had a long life. Château Lafite experimented with ground-glass stoppers in the 1820s but it was difficult to extract them without breaking the bottle itself, and from this time on cork had no real challengers. The turn of the twentieth century, though, saw an array of new stoppers.

CORK COMES AGAIN

Corks were introduced on a wider scale in the seventeenth century. In Act III, Scene ii of Shakespeare's *As You Like It* (1599), Rosalind entreats Celia (who is dressed as a man) to 'take the cork out thy mouth'. The first mention of a corkscrew appears to be in 1681, though the first patent was not granted until 1795 – the Reverend

Samuel Henshall's application for 'a new method of constructing and improving corkscrews' was patent no. 2061.

It was cork stoppers, combined with the stronger bottles created by Sir Kenelm Digby, an English diplomat and writer, that allowed the deliberate encouragement of secondary fermentation in the wines of Champagne in seventeenth-century England, a few years before Dom Pérignon's apocryphal but supposedly epoch-making call to his monastic colleagues: 'Come quickly for I am seeing stars.' However, though the cork has had thousands of years of history, its end may be in sight.

THE DEATH OF THE CORK

The incidence of corked wine – that is, wine that has been contaminated by TCA – is a subject of great debate. TCA is the wine industry's abbreviation for the chemical compound 2,4,6-trichloro-anisole. Corked wine, which has nothing whatsoever to do with bits of cork floating in your glass, tastes flat and smells like musty cellars or damp cardboard, though TCA is completely harmless.

Every wine authority will give a different figure on the numbers of bottles produced that are corked. The lowest accepted figure is around 5 per cent – one bottle in twenty. Estimates range as high as

one bottle in five. At the 2004 Sydney Royal Wine Show, 180 out of 2,160 bottles were affected. That's one in twelve. Part of the reason for this variation is that individual drinkers have different levels of sensitivity to corked wine. Another reason is that cork of different quality has vastly different levels of susceptibility. British wine authority Hugh Johnson has urged readers of his annual *Pocket Wine Book* to buy synthetic stoppers for their 'daily wines'. His experience is that 5 to 10 per cent of wines with cork stoppers are tainted.

For this reason a lot of research is going into alternative closures, while opinions about corks are becoming increasingly divisive. As Nigel Greening, owner of the acclaimed Felton Road vineyard in New Zealand, says, 'Why stick a bit of dead tree in your wine?' The loss of the cork would, however, create a problem in Bordeaux nomenclature. The term *aristocrate du bouchon* (literally 'aristocracy of the cork') is used to identify members of the old wine-trading families and differentiate them from the French noblemen who own the estates. This has not stopped many wine-producing countries from moving over to newer stoppers.

New Stoppers

With one-sixth of the world's wine now sealed with synthetic closures, one of the prime candidates to replace cork is the screw cap. The first patent was taken out by Dan Rylands of Barnsley, South Yorkshire, in 1889. The current favourite screw-cap closure is the 'Stelvin', developed by French firm Pechiney. It is consistent, effective and approximately the same price as natural cork. Fresh, young white wines clearly appear to benefit from the Stelvin, but the jury is still out over older, high-class reds. Will they age as effectively? No one knows for sure, although questions have been raised about possible negative effects. A tasting conducted at the University of Dijon, France, in 2004 by Professor Michel Feuillat compared two bottles of 1964 Nuits-Saint-Georges. One had a screw cap, the other a traditional cork. There was no clear difference between the two. The first Bordeaux Cru Classé to be stoppered with the Stelvin was the 2003 Graves of Château Couhins-Lurton.

The Guala Seal Elite is yet another new closure system. Developed by an Italian firm, it claims to allow a small amount of oxygen to enter the wine to prevent the development of reductive aromas that some claim spoil the wine when no oxygen is present.

BUT DO YOU NEED OXYGEN?

An Australian study conducted in 2005 by Allen Hart, Southcorp's winemaker, concluded that 'oxygen [is] not a vital component for the ongoing evolution and maturation of these red wines after bottling.' Small amounts of oxygen accelerate the evolution of a wine but are not necessary for it.

SCREWED

A Houston restaurant now has a section on its wine list for 'Alternative Closures'. However, what sommeliers (wine waiters) have not yet worked out is how to open screw caps with an appropriate level of ritual. Simply unscrewing and pouring lacks an opportunity for displaying erudition, judgement and gravitas. The best to date is to 'unscrew it as slowly as possible.' The same group of sommeliers did however have an answer to the question of what to call a TCA-tainted screw-cap wine (it can happen). You've guessed it . . . The slogan for one manufacturer of alternative stoppers is 'Twisted but not screwed,' which may provide an additional clue.

THE LOGIC OF SCREWING – RANDALL GRAHM'S REASONS FOR SWITCHING

Randall Grahm, an American wine producer, owner of Bonny Doon Vineyards and wit for whom the term 'eccentric' might have been coined, cited ten reasons for switching to screw caps:

1. Never pay corkage fees again.
2. When celebrating significant occasions with one's colleagues (parole, commutation of sentence), it's often difficult to locate a corkscrew.
3. 'Reverse' chic is just so in.
4. Can begin a conversational gambit with waitress with the line, 'Would you, err, unscrew my bottle?'
5. Perfect beverage for clothing-optional events.
6. Will never fall for the old 'left-handed corkscrew' gag again.
7. Hard to find corkscrews down by the railroad tracks.
8. Extremely humorous back-label can be pressed into service at occasional lulls in the conversation.
9. You can no longer be accused of being a cork-sniffer.
10. You will never again experience the heartbreak of TCA.

Another advantage of the screw cap is that it is 100 per cent tamper proof. Wine producers have long used foils, capsules and ribbons or paper strips over the neck and cork to ensure that wines cannot easily be tampered with, but these methods are open to abuse. All that such devices prevent is adulteration after distribution.

WINE FLAVOURINGS

Unfortunately, consumers have been screwed by producers – in many ways and over many centuries.

Producers (and in some eras, consumers) have always been prone to adding flavour to wine. Flavourings mask taste, add interest, or alcohol, correct over-aggressive acidity and, in some cases, extend life.

Period	*Ingredient(s) added*	*Purpose*
Ancient Egypt	Resin	Amphorae were coated with resin to prevent spoilage and improve flavour.
Ancient Egypt	Coriander	An aphrodisiac.
Crete – 2nd to 6th century BC	Crocus (as well as herbs)	Along with other ingredients, such as pepper, it was thought to cure asthma, obstinacy and insomnia.
Ancient Egypt and Rome	Honey	To sweeten wine and improve flavour. Often used in *mulsum* – cheap wine served free to the plebs at Roman public events.
Roman Empire – 1st century AD	Lead	A preservative that stopped fermentation, and which disguised inferior vintages. The lead in the ceramic glazes of imported wine jars was also a contributory source. Caused gout and sterility in men, infertility in women, and imbecility in both sexes. Peasants, who generally drank from goatskins, were far less affected.

Period	Ingredient(s) added	Purpose
Roman Empire	Sea water	Added to the roughest, sourest, end-of-pressing wine as part of the ingredients of *posca*, the staple drink of Roman legionnaires (a sort of classical Red Bull). The sponge lifted to Jesus's lips when he was on the Cross was soaked in *posca* in order to prolong his agony. Sea water was also used as a preservative in sweet Cretan wine.
Roman Empire	*Garum* (rotten-fish sauce), garlic, onion	Flavour improvers!
France – 19th century	Rhône wines from Hermitage	Added to Bordeaux wines to improve flavour and colour.
France – 1930s	Red wine from Algeria, southern France and Spain	Used to beef up Bordeaux and Burgundy. The catalyst for the development of the *Appellation d'Origine Contrôlée* (AOC) system.
Austria – 1985	Diethylene glycol (a component of antifreeze)	Used to improve sugar and alcohol levels and hence the classification and price. Only discovered when a producer tried to reclaim the VAT and aroused the suspicion of the tax collector.
South Africa – 2004	Green-pepper essence and piracine (a natural flavouring)	To enhance Sauvignon Blanc produced by KWV (a South African producer dominant since the early twentieth century). Two 'rogue' winemakers were fired. Under South African law they could have received up to four years in jail, but both now have been re-employed in the wine industry.

THE CORPSE OF MONSIEUR THIERRY BOUCHON . . .

In October 2002, Randall Grahm held a wake for the death of the cork. Jancis Robinson MW delivered the eulogy at Grand Central Station in New York. She extolled M. Bouchon's 'jolly good run' but warned 'how ridiculous it is when the most hideously tainted wines can be topped by perfectly sweet-smelling corks, and the most divine wines emerge from under a stink-bomb of a cork.'

There was an all-black menu created by chef Alison Kirsch that started with 'Blackened Almonds', progressed through 'Seared Black Cod with Miso' and concluded with 'Chocolate Coffin of Truffles and Jellies'. The 'cadaver' of the cork was displayed in a specially commissioned casket.

THE OAK INFLUENCE

Today's primary flavour-changer is oak, along with the other woods, such as chestnut, that are used for barrels. The supply of oak for casks has been dominated for centuries by the French, with the close-grained oaks of the Allier and Nevers *départements* in central France as long-established kings of the forest. But supplies are diminishing and eventually producers will need to turn to other sources. Oak from other sources, however, has different characteristics, which relate to the species of tree rather than the geographical origin of the wood. *Quercus sessiliflora* and *Quercus robur* are the key French species, while *Quercus alba* is the American standard bearer.

Oak source	Flavour contribution
Russia	More aromatic, brings out the fruit. High levels of vanillin but harsher and more drying on the finish.
Hungary	Creamy vanilla with more coconut flavours. Softer tannins than American oak.
France	Smooth and subtle.
USA	Obvious vanillin flavours – can be more astringent than European oaks.
Slovenia	High tannins (much used by Italian producers of the north-west).
Canada	Fennel and liquorice notes.
Germany	Nutty and toasty.

There are significant price differences between oaks from different sources. French oak barrels cost around €600 (£415) (though this can rise to €700 (£480) or more for top-quality wood) while American barrels are around half this price.

According to some experts, the major determinant of flavour is not so much the type of oak but the type and degree of its toasting.

As the wood is heated over a fire so different aromas are formed. The basic split is between light, medium and heavy toast. Lighter toasts emphasize fruit while heavier toasting produces more smoky, woody and spicy flavours.

BARRELS AND CHIPS

For the record, 'oak aged' and 'aged in oak' do not mean the same thing. 'Aged in oak' refers to a wine aged in oak barrels. 'Oak aged' means no barrels have been involved in the maturation process, but that the wine has had oak chips suspended in the vat, or that oak essence has been added. This practice is illegal in many countries, including those of the European Union. It is nonetheless widely practised and accounts for the overpowering but somehow disconnected sweet 'oakiness' typical of cheaper New World Chardonnays.

WINE AND LEAD

As with oak, so with lead. It adds flavour and sweetness and helps to preserve the wine. Unfortunately, it also poisons those who drink the wine. Lead poisoning from wine dates back at least to Roman times. Part of the Roman winemaking practice was to concentrate the grape juice by boiling it in lead cauldrons, which they discovered gave the wine a sweet taste. Pliny sanctioned this practice and it continued throughout the Middle Ages into the eighteenth century. It was only through the work of Dr Eberhard Göckel in the late seventeenth century that the pernicious effects of lead (including fever, constipation, acute stomach cramps, blindness and paralysis) were documented. According to Hugh Johnson, however, it still took until the late nineteenth century before the French ceased to use musket balls to sweeten wine.

THE FIRST FABLED VINTAGE

A wine that almost certainly was flavoured with lead was the first great vintage in recorded history.

The Falernian wine of 121 BC was the first vintage to achieve near-eternal fame. Falernian was a full-bodied white wine made from the Aminean grape grown near Naples. It was high in alcohol (perhaps 15 to 16 per cent) and was aged for twenty years or more until it had the colour of amber. Trimalchio, the rich slave of Petronius Arbiter's comedy the *Satyricon*, serves Falernian wine at his dinner party to show how far he has come up in the world. The wine was reputedly served to Caligula 160 years later (a tough test) and tasted by Pliny the Younger in AD 80. By then it was, he says, barely drinkable because it had become so concentrated.

THE COMET VINTAGE

The most famous of all the comet vintages was 1811. The astronomical body in question was Flaugergues's Comet (identified by Honoré Flaugergues), and the weather was perfect, which many attributed to the beneficial effect of the heavenly body that they could constantly see in the sky. It was a hot, dry summer (after a number of bad years since the turn of the century) and a great year for a range of wines. The 1811 Château d'Yquem was rated as a 100-pointer by Robert Parker in 1995. The stars on bottles of cognac originated as homage to the 1811 cognac vintage – one of the greatest ever. Other 'comet' years, including 1985 and 1989, are similarly celebrated, and in 1985 Château Lafite-Rothschild placed a comet on the label in homage to their great cosmic predecessor of 1811.

The comet vintage makes several literary appearances. Ernst Jünger's *Marmorklippen* (*On the Marble Cliffs*) has its hero and his brother drink wine made in the 'year of the comet'. The author claimed the wine he had in mind was Lafite 1811 (which he himself had never had the opportunity to drink). In Arthur Conan Doyle's 'The Stockbroker's Clerk', Dr Watson compares Holmes to a 'connoisseur who has just taken his first sip of a comet vintage.' This information, along with other data, is used by the French Sherlock Holmes Society to justify their 1999 claim that Holmes was, in fact, French. After all, he refused a knighthood (in 'The Adventure of the Three Garridebs') but accepted the Légion d'Honneur (in 'The Adventure of the Golden Pince-Nez'). He spoke perfect French and, disguised as a French labourer, he saved Watson from a beating in Montpellier. He drinks not just wine of the comet vintage but also Beaune and Montrachet.

COMET CHAMPAGNE

It is possible that the first 'modern' champagne was a 'comet' champagne. The secret of modern champagne production, discovered by Veuve Clicquot's team in the early nineteenth century, was that of *remuage* – a process of collecting and disgorging the yeast sediment by periodically turning and shaking the bottle – producing a clear rather than cloudy liquid. In 1814, Madame Clicquot's top salesman, M. Bohne, arrived in Russia shortly after Napoleon's retreat from Moscow. He was selling 1811 champagne and, according to his memoirs, queues formed outside his hotel room to taste this most 'limpid' (i.e. sediment-free) wine.

THE 'VICTORY VINTAGE'

Despite the widespread disruption of the war years, 1945 was an outstanding vintage. Michael Broadbent rates it as better than 1961. Bordeaux in particular had a stellar year. The wine was produced from mature, ungrafted vines and a severe May frost resulted in a small crop which was able to survive an extremely hot summer. Broadbent dubbed the Mouton-Rothschild 'a Churchill of wine' in recognition of its larger-than-life character. The Mouton label was produced by Philippe Jullian, a young French designer and artist, and was headed 'L'Année de la Victoire'. It incorporated Churchill's famous 'V for Victory' gesture (see page 56).

Though both red and white Bordeaux were superb that year, other parts of Europe benefited as well, though the hot summer favoured red wines rather than white. Burgundy and Rhône reds were magnificent. So too was port, despite (or because of) a year of drought. There were only twelve inches of rain in the year from

September 1944 to the end of August 1945. Alsace whites and German whites were equally fine – though the crops, not surprisingly, were tiny and very few examples are now to be found.

THE MILLENNIUM VINTAGE

The year 2000 was a wonderful year across much of Europe. Aided no doubt by the hype of the Millennium, prices for Bordeaux wine sold *en primeur* (that is, pre-bottling) reached record levels – as much as 75 per cent over 1999. An anonymous letter circulated at the trade show Vinexpo by merchants from London, Paris, New York and Los Angeles accused the first growths of committing 'retail genocide' with such extraordinary price rises.

In Europe, the year started cold and dry with plenty of rain in late spring and early summer. After the third week of July, however, the sun shone continuously – though not ferociously – through to harvest in late September.

Conditions were perfect for Bordeaux – with the sad exception of Sauternes where September rains spoiled the party – and Robert Parker rated the year 2000 as the greatest vintage ever. The *Wine Spectator* agreed: they claimed it to be the 'vintage of a lifetime'. Some Bordeaux wine bought *en primeur* in 2001 has gained nearly 200 per cent in value in the four years since. Not, evidently, as genocidal as was first thought.

ROTHSCHILD AND THE ART OF THE LABEL

The Victory Vintage label was the first of Baron Philippe de Rothschild's now celebrated series.

In 1945 Rothschild initiated an annual commission for the upper band of the label. He persuaded artists of increasing renown (including Picasso, Francis Bacon and Keith Haring) to produce the labels for Château Mouton-Rothschild. The series started in 1945 and a complete run of the labels from 1945 to 1994 fetched $38,000 (£22,000) at auction in 1996. It is now on show at the Royal York Hotel in Toronto.

The artists receive no money for their work – just four cases of Mouton-Rothschild, which is worth at least $7,500 (£4,300) in today's money. They get two cases of 'their' wine and two of another vintage. Marc Chagall (1970), Andy Warhol (1975) and John Huston (1982) were winning vintage years. Losers, at least in terms of the wine quality in 'their' year, include Pablo Picasso (1973), Salvador Dalí (1958) and Joan Miró (1969). The most recent label (2002) is by Russian conceptual artist Ilya Kabakov.

The artists' primary brief is to be 'colourful' so as to contrast with the dark colours of wine and bottle, and the dark red and black of the lettering. Three themes are allowed as inspiration: the ram, symbol of the château and subject of the very first label that Baron Philippe had commissioned in 1924; the vine and the vineyard; and the pleasures of drinking wine.

Since 1945 only three vintages have not had an artist-designed label: 1953, 1977 and 2000.

1953 was the *Année du Centenaire* of the purchase of the Mouton-Rothschild property. A portrait of the founder was used on the label.

In 1977, Queen Elizabeth, the Queen Mother, stayed at Mouton and the year's vintage was dedicated to her.

In 2000, the label was enamelled in gold with a reproduction of the Augsburg Ram, a famous silver-gilt drinking cup crafted by a German master metalsmith in 1590, and now an exhibit in the château's Museum of Wine in Art.

WINE LABELS

Wine labels themselves have been around since the end of the seventeenth century, although the necessary glues to hold them firmly in place were a mid-nineteenth-century development. Labels were unnecessary until wine was sold and served in bottles. The English diplomat Sir Kenelm Digby was probably the first to create more robust bottles that could be used for the storage of wine, and which replaced the simple carafes of frail glass that needed to be packed in straw to survive. It would be fair to say that Chianti bottles did once need those straw cases that we all love to hate ...

Silver neck-labels to aid identification of the wine within were hung on carafes from the mid-seventeenth century. Alternatively, the seals of either the merchant or the owner were impressed in the molten glass, since bottles were often made to order.

The First Paper Label

The first paper label appears to have been written by the Italian botanist Pier Antonio Micheli around 1700 to identify his bottle of Verdicchio, which was the only word on the label. Paper (or parchment) labels were tied round the necks of early champagne bottles with a note to indicate the year and the place of origin. By the middle of the eighteenth century, the responsibility for labelling the wine had passed to the producer. These early labels – printed in black type on white paper – were used by producers such as Claude Moët (the forerunner of Moët & Chandon). They listed only the name of the wine and the year of the vintage.

The invention of lithography by the Austrian Alois Senefelder in 1798 revolutionized the production of labels and label design. Drawings could be incorporated, colour could be used, and short and large print runs could be set in motion.

Labels with a Message

Bartolo Mascarello, a Barolo producer known as the 'Last of the Mohicans' for his severely traditional views, hand-painted his own labels. Probably the most famous was 'No Barrique, No Berlusconi,' created just before the Italian general election in 2002 and displayed in a wineshop in Alba. The label showed a brick wall with the scrawled message and a portrait of Italy's Prime Minister, Silvio Berlusconi, smirking. Mascarello was a fierce opponent of both –

though he failed to prevent either Berlusconi's re-election, or the steady influx of *barriques* (small barrels of new French oak that internationalized the traditional style of the wine) into the cellars of Barolo that once had held only the vast *botti* (casks) of Slovenian oak. On another label he invoked the spirit of Robespierre by demanding that wood should be used for barricades rather than *barriques*. Sadly, Mascarello died in March 2005.

LABELS WITH A FUNCTION

The magazine *Time* recorded as one of its 'Coolest Inventions 2004' a temperature-sensitive label. The label on the Mar de Frades, a crisp Albariño produced on the north-west coast of Spain, is printed in heat-sensitive ink. When the bottle is appropriately chilled a small blue ship appears on top of the symbolic waves on the label. The label was developed by the British company, William Grant & Sons. Another use of this technology is to display a woman who is clothed at room temperature and naked when chilled (which sounds somewhat counter-intuitive).

SCANDALOUS LABELS

Since 1997 the Italian wine producer Alessandro Lunardelli has specialized in wine labels that shock. Mussolini wine was his first, with labels showing Il Duce in dramatic poses. Depending on whom you believe, the wine appeals either to collectors of kitsch, or right-wingers nostalgic for a golden past. Lunardelli rejects the latter interpretation, pointing out that he also offers bottles bearing images of Che Guevara, Lenin and Stalin. Sales, however, were modest until his Hitler label (bearing the slogan, 'One People, One Empire, One Leader') was banned by the EC and the German government.

Mao Tse-Tung Merlot

Stalin's face also appears on a wine produced in the Ukraine. This was banished from Canadian shelves by the fury of the thousands of Canadians of Ukrainian extraction who moved to Canada after the Second World War to escape the dictator. Their spokesman said: 'I don't think anyone in Canada would welcome a Hitler Riesling or a Stalin Sherry or a Pol Pot Port or a Mao Tse-Tung Merlot.'

In 2002 a Portuguese producer was forced to withdraw 25,000 cases of Esporão when their wine, which bore a label of a bearded man who closely resembled Osama bin Laden, appeared on the American market in mid-September 2001. Not the best timing, it must be said.

Paint It Red

Frenchman Philippe Dufrenoy paints with wine. His preferred medium is Grand Cru red wines and his conversion to wine painting came from testing some newly acquired brushes after lunch in a Bordeaux bistro. Different wines give different colours, with Syrah and Pomerol offering 'extraordinary nuances'. His speciality is portraits of wine men and women painted with their own product. Robert Mondavi has been immortalized with Opus One and Gérard Perse with Château Pavie.

BRAILLE LABELS

Michael Chapoutier, who calls himself a vine-grower (the description on his business card), is the seventh-generation head of Maison M. Chapoutier, possibly the greatest of all producers of the northern Rhône and owner of around 25 per cent of the great hill of Hermitage. Since 1995, all of his labels can be read by the blind as they are printed in Braille. The inspiration for this decision came from a meeting with blind musician Ray Charles, but Chapoutier has other reasons to acknowledge the contribution of the blind to his business. Eight hectares of his Hermitage holding were bequeathed to him by Monier de la Sizeranne, a local landowner who had been blinded in a shotgun accident.

THE WINE NAMES OF RANDALL GRAHM

Grahm, owner of Bonny Doon Vineyards in California and founder of the Rhone Rangers (a non-profit organization 'established to advance the public's knowledge of Rhône grapes . . . grown in America'), is also famous for his labels and his punned names. (He also has more Google hits for 'eccentric winemaker' than any other individual.)

Grahm's stated beliefs are:

＊ Wine should be as much fun as government regulations allow.

* Great wine starts in the vineyard.
* We should champion the strange, esoteric, ugly-duckling grape varieties of the world.

Current and past offerings include:

Name	Wine
Big House Red	Syrah, Petite Syrah, Carignan plus Grenache, Barbera, Malbec and others.
Big House Pink	Cariganno, Charbono, Zinfandel and several others.
Le Cigare Volante	Grenache, Syrah, Mourvèdre.
Le Cigare Blanc	Primarily Roussanne (97%).
Old Telegram	Old Vine Mourvèdre.
Cardinal Zin	Zinfandel (from 'Beastly Old Vines').
Il Fiasco	Sangiovese.
Heart of Darkness	67% Tannat, 33% Cabernet Sauvignon.

Le Cigare Volante ('The Flying Cigar') takes its name from an incident in 1954 in which the local council issued an edict stating that spaceships were not to land in the Châteauneuf-du-Pape vineyards in their bailiwick. The labels confirm the eccentricity – and memorability – of the names.

SGT PEPPER'S RHONELY HEARTS CLUB BAND

Randall Grahm's rock opera celebrating the wines of the Rhône premiered in 2004 before an audience of over 250 journalists and distributors. For $20,000 (£11,500) spent on producing the opera, Grahm received heavy-duty press coverage for *Born to Rhone* – an indication of how marketing-smart this particular Californian eccentric is. The opera was his own composition, and featured acrobats, a contortionist, a naked juggler and satirical songs.

As well as songs promoting the Rhône, such as 'Why Don't We Do It In The Rhône?' (to the tune of the Beatles' 'Why Don't We

Do It In The Road?'), Grahm took digs at critics, the *Wine Spectator* and, of course, Chardonnay:

> *How can critics be so clueless?*
> *How can critics be so cruel?*
> *Easy to make Chard,*
> *Easy to ferment cold.*

Grahm's combination of smart marketing and serious winemaking has led to consistent sales growth of over 20 per cent per year, and the company now turns out more than a third of a million cases per year.

CELEBRITY WINE (DECEASED)

Aside from Hitler, Mussolini and the other famous (or infamous) individuals commemorated on the labels of Alessandro Lunardelli's wines, a number of celebrities have been immortalized – if that's the correct word – by winemakers.

Winston Churchill's deep attachment to Pol Roger champagne earned him a posthumous black border on the labels of his favourite champagne, which was renamed as Cuvée Sir Winston Churchill.

THE GRAPEFUL DEAD

Jerry Garcia, late frontman of the Grateful Dead, is commemorated on the labels of J. Garcia varietal wines from the Clos du Bois winery in Sonoma County, California. Jerry was not a wine drinker (preferring other stimulants) but the first shipment of 22,000 cases sold out in just a month in early 2004. Each of the wines is decorated with one of the five hundred or so abstract paintings that Garcia produced in the final ten years of his life.

ELVIS HITS THE BOTTLE

Signature Wines of California produce a 'Graceland Cellars Line', which includes a Blue Suede Chardonnay, a King Cabernet Sauvignon and a Jailhouse Red Merlot. CEO Scott Cahill said the company was 'very proud' of the wines. 'Our wineries have worked hard to put the same care into our wines that Elvis put into his music. We think fans of wine and Elvis will agree.'

MARILYN MERLOT

Fellow star Marilyn Monroe gets a rather different treatment. The 1985 Marilyn Merlot (described by critics as 'a decent Californian Merlot') is on the market for $3,500 (£2,000). Produced each year is a new wine, a new label and a new Marilyn pose. The current (2004) wine retails for $25 (£14). The venture began in the mid-1980s as 'a light-hearted approach to the wine business [that] became a serious wine and a serious Marilyn collectable,' according to the Nova Wines Partners website. Royalties go to Anna Strasberg, who helps to support the Lee Strasberg Theatre (which taught Marilyn the 'Method'), as well as to the Anna Freud Foundation's children's treatment centre. Nova Wines have also launched a slightly younger Merlot under the Norma Jean name, with pictures of Marilyn as a brunette before she became the more familiar sensual blonde.

WINE AND SEX

Wine and sex have been inextricably linked, possibly since Noah exposed himself after drinking too deep of the products of his newly harvested vines (Genesis 9:20–7).

Women in ancient Sparta were not allowed to drink wine. This prohibition did not apply in Athens, where a woman named Cleo was, according to the playwright Aristophanes, accustomed to drinking all the men under the table.

In thirteenth-century Vienna, the local wine bars (housed in the local cellars) were notorious as the haunts of harlots. Consequently, in 1403, the authorities banned the wine bars, though not the ladies of the night. This injunction seems to have affected neither trade, if the edicts of the subsequent centuries are anything to go by. In 1572, the authorities took the radical step of banning women from working in a dual capacity as harlots and wine-bar waitresses. In 1741, the City Guard was dissolved after the *Batzenhausen* in the bastions of the city wall had intermingled the wine and sex trades too closely.

CLEAVAGE CREEK AND NAKED NYMPHETS

More recently, a Californian winery produced a 'jug wine' under the 'Cleavage Creek' brand. The label personifies the assets in question with the justification that the wine is produced from the 'cleavage of the most beautiful Californian hills'. It will also, so they say, 'seduce your palate'. No tasting notes are known, but 10 per cent of profits are donated to breast-cancer research.

A rather classier wine almost failed to reach the US market after the Bureau of Alcohol, Tobacco and Firearms (ATF) banned a drawing by Balthus (Balthazar Klossowski de Rola) of a naked nymphet on the label of the 1993 Mouton-Rothschild.

It was sold with a blank where the image should have been. The blank label is now a valuable collectable. It does not, however, conform in any way to the stylistic guidelines for labels laid down by Philippe de Rothschild (see page 49).

NAKED LADIES AND SKELETAL RIPOSTES

The ATF also banned a 1975 label by the prolific and in no way puritanical US artist David Lance Goines. The label, for the Kenwood Winery, featured a naked female figure reclining amidst hillside vines. It was promptly declared 'obscene or indecent'. Goines's next attempt featured not the woman but rather her skeleton, but this too was banned and Kenwood marketed the bottle showing only the hillside vines. Twenty-two years later the label was resubmitted for approval. This time it passed the ATF's test (though the Ohio Board of Alcohol Control continued to object to its 'offensive' nature), and over 3,000 cases sold out – fast.

'A Leetle Bit of Imagination . . . '

On a slightly different, but not unrelated, note, Michael Broadbent, in *Vintage Wines: Fifty Years of Tasting Three Centuries of Wine*, tells the story of veteran Napa Valley winemaker André Tchelistcheff tasting an 1898 Château Lafite.

'After opening and decanting, André, with the microphone full on, but as if to himself in a charming French-Russian accent, took a sip and said, "Tasting old wine is like making love to an old lady." The whole room went silent; he [Tchelistcheff] paused. "It is possible." Another pause. "It can even be enjoyable." Sip and pause again, adding: "But it requires a leetle bit of imagination."'

The Joy of Wine

A 2004 *Wine Magazine* survey of its readers placed wine above sex as *the* unmissable pleasure. The answers to the question 'What would be most difficult to give up for a month?' were:

35 per cent wine
29 per cent sex
15 per cent caffeine
11 per cent television
5 per cent chocolate

3 per cent shopping
2 per cent golf

Another survey, this time conducted by researchers at Glasgow University, concluded that the most effective way to increase the attractiveness of a prospective partner is to consume two glasses of wine, which improves the perceived beauty of the opposite sex by around 25 per cent.

THE GAY MARKET

Several wineries and several wines have attempted to gain a major share of the gay market. Nevada's Rainbow Ridge Wines featured a rainbow-coloured grape cluster on their 2001 Alicante Bouschet (the recipient of 90 Parker points).

In the USA, 60 per cent of gay and lesbian consumers buy premium wine every month, but it has been estimated that their total consumption could be trebled if one or more wine brands took the market seriously, in the way that Absolut (makers of vodka) did with its strong showing in the gay media and in its commissioning of gay artists to execute advertising campaigns.

On the other side of the world, Pansy! Rosé, produced by New Zealand winemakers Kim and Erica Crawford, is explicitly targeted at the gay market, and is worth $50 million (£30 million) annually in Australia and New Zealand. The wine, made from Merlot, Cabernet Franc and a small amount of late-harvest Chardonnay, and described by Erica Crawford as 'fresh, funky and fun', was initially launched in Auckland in 2002 but hit Sydney in late 2004. The wine is also a steady seller in the USA.

SEX – THE WINE

Californian winemaker Larry Mawby makes a sparkling wine called simply 'Sex' as part of his M. Lawrence label. He was, he says, astonished when the ATF gave their permission to the labelling, indeed, so astonished that he 'nearly spilled coffee all over himself'. The wine has won plaudits from very discriminating palates. After a tasting of  Michigan wines in 2004, Jancis Robinson MW wrote approvingly to Tom Stevenson, the event's organizer, to say that she was 'really impressed by that Sex', and praising its balance compared to other sparkling wines at the tasting. The wine – a value-priced dry pink sparkler – is part of a range that includes Fizz (a demi-sec) and US (a brut). The wines are made from excess Californian wine (mostly Pinot Noir), and Mawby re-ferments them by the 'charmat', or 'tank', method (where the wine is fermented and the bubbles created inside pressurized tanks rather than in the bottle).

TOASTS – HOW IT ALL BEGAN

Wine has always involved the celebration of hedonism. Though the first mention of the term 'to toast' goes back to the sixteenth century, the near-naked girls on Egyptian drinking vessels and the drinking games of the Greeks and Romans make it clear that celebrating the charms of the opposite sex (or even of the same sex) has long been a part of the ritual of drinking.

For once, Falstaff, in Shakespeare's *The Merry Wives of Windsor*, is seen in practical rather than lecherous guise when he asks for his jug of sack to have 'toast put in't'. The charcoal in toasted bread reduced the acidity of wine and hence improved the flavour. The practice itself appears to go back to Roman or even Greek times.

From a method of improving the taste of the wine, in the late seventeenth century the term 'toast' evolved to refer to the practice of celebrating one's fellow drinkers, friends, notables and worthies. The *Oxford English Dictionary* suggests that the practice originated in naming a lady whose name the company was asked to celebrate – on the basis that her name would flavour the wine just as the spiced toast in the wine had originally done. Such celebrations were led by a 'toastmaster' who benefited from having a glass with a thicker base and thicker walls, so while it would appear full it actually held far less liquid than a standard glass.

The toastmaster's role was to ensure that all present had an equal chance to toast and be toasted. Once all the guests had been toasted (and it was a deadly insult to omit anyone), then absent friends and celebrated beauties would take centre stage. The phrase 'the toast of the town' dates back to this point and to this custom.

SHOES AND CHAMPAGNE

From the late eighteenth century also comes the first mention of drinking to the health of a lady (to use a polite term) from her shoe. Hugh Johnson cites an item in the *Connoisseur* of June 1754: 'some bloods being in company with a celebrated *fille de joie*, one of them pulled off her shoe, and in excess of gallantry filled it with champagne, and drank it off to her health.' That same (evidently boisterous) evening saw the lady's shoe being cooked for the consumption of the assembled company. The cook, one Tom Pierce, named it 'Le Soulier à la Murphy' after the mistress of Louis XIV.

Olga Beruti, a fourth-generation Parisian bootmaker, recommends Veuve Clicquot's La Grande Dame champagne as a shoe polish – despite the champagne costing over £70 a bottle. The alcohol is said to give a better final finish to the shoe than water.

Attempts were made to tone down the custom of the toast, whose primary purpose was to encourage drinking to excess. Nineteenth-century toasting practices were far more decorous – focused on patriotic sentiment rather than individual celebration.

TOASTS

An ENGLISH toast of the Middle Ages:
*May your love be like good wine, and grow stronger
as it grows older.*

A GROUCHO MARX toast:
I drink to your charm, your beauty and your brains –
which gives you a rough idea of how hard up I am for a drink.

A GERMAN toast:
Wasser ist billig, rein und gut; Doch verdunt es unser Blut.
Water is cheap, pure and good; but it thins the blood.

ANONYMOUS:
As you slide down the banister of life,
may the splinters never point the wrong way.

A toast by LORD BYRON:
Let us have wine and women, mirth and laughter
Sermons and soda water the day after.

On being asked to toast the unmentionable (a hundred years ago)
subject of 'sex', GEORGE BERNARD SHAW stood and said only:
It gives me great pleasure.

An ANONYMOUS MEDIEVAL toast:
Gaudeamus igitur
Iuvenes dum sumus.
Post iucundam juventutes
Post molestam senectutem
Nos habebit humus.

Let us then rejoice,
While we are young.
After the happiness of youth,
And the annoyances of age,
The earth will claim us.

Although the earth will claim us all in the end, there is good
evidence that regular drinking, in moderate amounts, will postpone,
or at least delay, the dread day.

HEALTH IN A GLASS (OR TWO) A DAY

*I have enjoyed great health at a great age because every day
since I can remember, I have consumed a bottle of wine except
when I have not felt well. Then I have consumed two bottles.*
Attributed to an anonymous BISHOP OF SEVILLE

Former US Secretary of State William M. Evarts (1818–1901) would
probably have agreed. Asked whether drinking a wide range of
'different' vintages affected his health and well-being, he replied,
'Not at all, madam, it's the *indifferent* wines that produce that result.'

TAKE TWO

Drinking two glasses of wine a day has been proven to benefit your
health. Wine's primary effect is on the blood – and hence on the
heart. Grape skins contain compounds called polyphenols that are
released during the winemaking process, acting as antioxidants, and
it now seems clear that these polyphenols account for the positive
health effects of wine. On one hand, they inhibit the formation of
cholesterol and hence lower the risk of IHD (ischaemic heart
disease), which is the biggest natural killer in the developed world.
Secondly, as antioxidants, polyphenols destroy free radicals and thus

slow the development of cancer. These findings by French scientist Serge Renaud sparked the 1990s boom in red wine (principally Merlot), particularly in the United States. He had solved the 'French paradox'. How was it that the French (as a general rule) consume lots of saturated fat, but live long and healthy lives?

RECIPE FOR LIFE?

Subsequent to Renaud's findings, scientists investigated other food and drink. A 2003 Australian study strongly suggested that a diet of fish, wine, fruit, vegetables, almonds, garlic and dark chocolate could increase life expectancy in men by more than six years. Women only get five years' benefit. The same two-glass limit (around 150 ml.) for wine applied and the limit for chocolate was 100 grams.

Wine (and beer) in moderation decreases the risk of peptic ulcers. And diabetes. And prostate cancer. Perhaps even the common cold. Wine also inhibits the development of dementia. But all these positive effects are dependent on moderate drinking. Above one or two glasses (to a maximum of 30 grams of alcohol) and the benefits disappear. In particular, excessive drinking causes problems in the liver, pancreas, kidneys and bowels. Those who should not consume any alcohol at all are pre-menopausal women with a family history of breast cancer. Women in the early stages of pregnancy are also strongly advised not to drink.

None of this – except perhaps the chocolate – would have surprised the ancient Greek doctors. The classical physicians Hippocrates and Galen used the antioxidants and alcohol in wines to prevent infection in wounds. In particular, Galen recommended a sweet red Cretan wine called Theraios. The ancient Egyptians used wine for a variety of medicinal purposes, which included purging the body of worms, treating asthma and acting as an enema. They did, however, mix the wine with a combination of gums, resins, herbs and spices – and a judicious admixture of animal dung and bird droppings.

SHOULD IT BE RED OR WHITE?

Red wine has long been seen as having more positive health benefits than white – levels of polyphenols are higher in red wine than in white wines because white grapes are deskinned after being crushed. However, according to an American study carried out by the University of Buffalo, New York, white wine improves lung function. It may also improve joint health. The active compounds of white wine appear to be smaller in molecular size and so are more easily absorbed into the bloodstream.

To put red back into the driving seat, London researchers believe that the resveratrol, one of the polyphenols found in red-grape skins, improves the body's ability to fight conditions such as emphysema and bronchitis. However, an inhaler is needed to ingest sufficient quantities. An Oregon vineyard has received US Federal authority to label the resveratrol content of its wines. Labels of the Willamette Valley Vineyards 2002 Vintage Selection Pinot Noir carry the text 'Pinot Noir develops a natural defence against botrytis [mould] in our moist, cool climate – the antioxidant resveratrol.' The Willamette wines have between 19 to 71 resveratrol molecules per litre of wine. Ten is considered high.

THE THINKERS' DRINK

A study of 6,000 British civil servants suggested – though did not prove – that the more wine you drink, the greater the cognitive benefits. Those drinking five bottles a week had the highest test results – covering intelligence, memory, vocabulary and fluency. The overall effect was greater for women than men.

HEALTHIER WINES

A French white wine called Paradoxe Blanc is deliberately enriched with antioxidants – the key to heart health. By changing the winemaking process (mashing the skins and increasing the skin contact) white wine can be given much higher levels of polyphenols and bioflavonoids than normal.

There is some evidence to suggest that the higher the altitude of the vineyard, the healthier the wine. Higher levels of UV light at altitude stimulates the synthesis of polyphenols. A study of Sardinian wine reached a similar conclusion, and pointed to the high number of centenarians in the Nuoro area as supporting evidence.

WINE ICE CREAM

A South African winery, working in conjunction with the Sinnfull ice-cream operator, has created a range of 'vine-therapy' ice creams. Grape extracts in the ice creams account for the health benefits that led Tony McKeever, the company MD, to say, 'Now you can eat ice cream and look younger at the same time.' The range includes, for example, Blackberry and Cherry Pinotage 2004. Since Pinotage grape seeds are high in antioxidants they provide a bigger boost to the immune system than standard doses of vitamin C.

WINE IN A PILL

Even if you hate the taste of wine you can mimic its health-giving effects with a pill. In the USA, Resveratrol Partners make such a pill; marketed under the name of Longevinex, it contains red wine molecules. A French company has done the same by extracting polyphenols from tannin-rich wines. The British pharmacy chain Boots stocked but rapidly de-listed a similar product. It is hard to be depressed by such evidence of good sense on the part of drinkers.

HEADACHES AND HANGOVERS

Dehydration is a primary cause of hangovers. Drink water along with your wine and you'll improve your chances of feeling better the next day.

For those unfortunate enough to get headaches whilst drinking, the probable cause is an individual reaction to the natural elements in wine. Phenolic flavonoids (found more in red wine than white) and tannins cause headaches in some individuals. All fermented products – including wine – also contain histamines and tyramines that either dilate or constrict blood vessels. Low-acid red wine is the worst culprit.

DEATH BY WINE

George Plantagenet, Duke of Clarence (1449–1478), is reputed to have chosen death by drowning in a butt of wine in the Tower of London. The story may be true. Chronicler Dominic Mancini first mentioned the story in his *The Usurpation of Richard III* just five years after Clarence's death. Mancini refers to a cask of 'sweet wine', and later writers interpreted this to be Malmsey wine from Crete. The Duke's brother, Richard of Gloucester (later Richard III), may have been responsible for Clarence's death. Much more likely is that the attribution of blame to Richard is one of Shakespeare's many prejudices.

DEATH BY WINE – ITALIAN STYLE

Moving on several hundred years to 1985, an Italian producer intent on a quick profit concocted a 'Barbera' from barrel ends and methanol (methyl alcohol). Either twenty or twenty-three people died (sources vary) as a result of that concoction, but it had almost no effect on the reputation of Italian wine as a whole, though it damaged somewhat the Barbera name.

DEATH AND RESURRECTION (BY ANTIFREEZE)

Somewhat more disastrous to the wine industry of a nation was the Austrian scandal of the same decade (see page 41). To accumulate a lethal dose of the antifreeze that was used to adulterate the wine would have required the consumption of around twenty-eight bottles of the wine a day for two weeks. The discovery of the crime, however, led to an 80-per-cent drop in sales and destroyed the reputation of Austrian wine for a decade. Such a setback had a happy ending, however. Perhaps from a determination to prove itself again, the Austrian wine industry now makes some of the finest wines in the world. In 2003, Austrian Grüner Veltliners and Chardonnays took seven of the top ten slots in the so-called Judgement of Vienna organized by Jancis Robinson MW and Tim Atkin MW. The Austrian wines beat some of the greatest names of Burgundy and California. The top wine was a 1990 Knoll Grüner Veltliner Smaragd. For Tim Atkin it confirmed his view that 'alongside Germany and France, Austria is one of the three great white wine producing countries on the planet.'

DEATHLY VINTAGES – 1

Hannibal Lector, the 'cannibal' of Thomas Harris's novels, was a connoisseur of both wine and death. In *The Silence of the Lambs*, Lector famously ate the liver of an over-bold census-taker with 'some fava beans and a nice Chianti'. In the sequel, *Hannibal*, Lector's fascination with the greatest white Burgundies and the finest Sauternes allows FBI Agent Clarice Starling to track him down. Château d'Yquem is, in the end, the instrument both of her capture by Dr Lector and their final, mutual seduction as Clarice allows Yquem to drip from her breast into his waiting mouth. It is unclear how the Comte de Lur-Saluces (whose family owned Château d'Yquem for many years) views this confirmation of the wine's seductive powers, but Parisian courtesans allegedly used the same technique. The website of Austrian wine-glass company Riedel devotes a page to working out which of their products Lector might have used. The conclusion is that it would be 400/55. It is unclear which of the Riedel glasses is used in the film, *Hannibal*.

DEATHLY VINTAGES – 2

Less well known is Tony Aspler's *A Wine Lover's Mystery* series. These self-published novels feature wine-writer Ezra Brant whose adventures are chronicled in *Blood is Thicker Than Beaujolais*, *The Beast of Barbaresco* and *Death on the Douro*. Another contemporary wine story is Nadia Gordon's *Sharp Shooter*, part of her *Napa Valley Mystery* series in which, according to the blurb, 'Napa Valley chef Sunny McCloskey launches her own investigation into the politics of the wine industry where she encounters a killer with evil designs for the area.' Another murder mystery set in this wine region is Laura Reese's *Panic Snap*, 'a story of extreme sexual obsession and one family's terrible secret.' This has a strong S&M theme, and isn't for the faint-hearted.

YQUEM AGAIN

Of a different literary class is Fyodor Dostoevsky's *The Devils* (also known as *The Possessed*). In this novel is the story of the suicide of a boy of nineteen. Entrusted with 400 roubles by his poor family, he 'squanders' the money in a gaming den. After a day drinking with the gypsies he returns to his hotel and asks for 'a cutlet, a bottle of Château d'Yquem and some grapes'. Having drunk half the Yquem he shoots himself in the heart with a 'little three-chambered revolver'. Those who find his body drink the remains of the wine. Callous, but understandable.

LIFE AFTER DEATH

Wine frequently accompanied mummified Egyptian pharaohs on their journey to the afterlife. Wine residues from the tomb of Tutankhamun suggest he was buried with numerous jars of red wine. The inscriptions on the jars proclaimed the name of the winemaker, Khaa, and the year, 5. Palm wine – rather than grape wine – was used to wash the bodies and organs to kill bacteria before mummification.

BYRON'S SKULL

Two other men obsessed by death and their posthumous reputations were Lord Byron and John Keats.

George Gordon Byron, the mad, bad 6th Lord Byron, was keen to demonstrate both his madness and his badness to the world. Although he was an enthusiast for spritzers (white wine mixed with soda water), he projected an image of decadence and excess. Both of these were supported by the story of his drinking cup. As his (somewhat embellished) tale goes: 'The gardener in digging

[discovered] a skull that had probably belonged to some jolly friar or monk of the abbey [Newstead Abbey, Byron's home] about the time it was dismonasteried. Observing it to be of giant size and in a perfect state of preservation, a strange fancy seized me of having it set and mounted as a drinking cup. I accordingly sent it to town and it returned with a very high polish and of a mottled colour like tortoise shell.' The cup cost 17 pounds and 17 shillings to set and Byron subsequently wrote a poem, 'Lines Engraved upon a Cup Formed from a Skull', which begins:

> *Start not – nor deem my spirit fled;*
> *In me behold the only skull,*
> *From which, unlike a living head,*
> *Whatever flows is never dull.*

John Keats

Keats, in 'Ode to a Nightingale', calls for a 'draught of vintage! that hath been Cool'd a long age in the deep-delvèd earth'. The poet's pleasure is a 'beaker of the warm South, Full of the true, the blushful Hippocrene, With beaded bubbles winking at the brim'. In Greek mythology, the Hippocrene was the name of a fountain of sparkling water brought forth by Pegasus's hoof striking the ground – not much blushfulness there. But why waste a good name? Hippocrene is also the name of a red Australian sparkling wine made from Shiraz with a dash of Cabernet Sauvignon and Malbec. In 1999 it was ranked in the top ten of Australian red sparkling wines by *Wine* magazine.

Keats was also notorious – perhaps unfairly – for covering his tongue with cayenne pepper in order to appreciate better 'the delicious coldness of claret in all its glory'. True or false, this story, retailed by rival poet Benjamin Robert Haydon, reminds us that room temperature in an unheated Georgian house was not the same as the average room temperature in the twenty-first century. In the eighteenth century wines were preferred cold. This would have helped to disguise the taste that may well have been tainted after the trip across Europe and the Channel in imperfectly cleaned barrels. For the record, many red wines benefit from being drunk cooler than current practice – Cabernet Franc wines from the Loire, in particular, are better cool.

CELEBRITY STUFF

From two nineteenth-century celebrities to the present day.

As high-earning entertainers (be it in sports, films or music) get older, hellraising loses its appeal and wine cellars become one of the accoutrements of a more mature (and wealthy) lifestyle. A small proportion even catches the bug to the extent of buying vineyards. Some – like Sting with his 180-hectare estate in Tuscany – remain content with producing and bottling for family use. His 40 hectares of top-rated Chianti vines alone will produce approximately 250,000 bottles of wine annually. Others, whether to exploit their celebrity, improve their tax position or simply because they can, take their chances in the open market.

Celebrity/Area	Wine	What they say
Greg Norman (golfer) South Australia	Greg Norman Estates Reserve Shiraz 1998	'Such a deep, intense flavour, filled with tannins that are pronounced but not overbearing, and a hint of blueberry. There is so much depth to this wine' – Greg Norman. 94 Parker points.

Celebrity/Area	*Wine*	*What they say*
Francis Ford Coppola (film director) California	Niebaum–Coppola Estate Winery	'America's Grand Wine Estate' – Niebaum–Coppola website. But they do get 90+ Parker points.
Gérard Depardieu (actor) France (Anjou and Bordeaux)	Château de Tigné	94 Parker points.
Sam Neill (actor) Central Otago, New Zealand	Two Paddocks Vineyard	'Awfully drinkable' – Sam Neill (but Jancis Robinson MW appears to agree).
Cliff Richard (singer) Algarve, Portugal	La Vida Nuova	Joanna Simon of the *Sunday Times*: 'If Sir Cliff Richard was a wine, he would surely be born-again Mateus Rosé – fresh-faced but bland, sweet and a little cloying.' La Vida Nuova was the fastest-selling product ever on Tesco.com – beating the DVD release of *Lord of the Rings* into second place.
Olivia Newton-John (singer/actress) South Australia and Riverlands, Australia	Koala Blue	'Koala Blue Adds Class to a Cheap Date' said the press release. The name was originally that of Olivia's chain of fashion boutiques but these went bust and the name was reborn as a wine, water and chocolate brand. It has had heavy exposure (and ridicule) on *The Simpsons*. She subsequently launched a limited-edition 'signature wine' – 'Olivia' – in 2004.

Celebrity/Area	Wine	What they say
Joe Montana (American-football player) Napa Valley, California	Beringer Vineyards Montagia	Twelve standard bottles and one 9-litre bottle made $210,000 (£120,000) at the 2000 Napa Valley auction.
Mario Andretti (racing driver) Napa Valley, California	Andretti Winery Cabernet Sauvignon	'Lush, delicious and hedonistic … impressive' – 92 Parker points.
Club Atlético Boca Juniors (football team) Argentina	Boca Premium	'An easy-drinking Cabernet Sauvignon retailing at $4 a bottle' – Boca Juniors.

FRANCIS FORD COPPOLA – DIRECTOR AND WINEMAKER

Coppola claims that film-making and winemaking are very similar – perhaps accounting for the number of actors with interests in vineyards. 'Each [films and wine] depends on source material and takes a lot of time to perfect. The big difference is that today's winemakers still worry about quality.'

He is deadly serious about the quality of *his* wine, at least. With his wife Eleanor, he bought the historic Inglenook Estate (at the time he was 'searching for a quaint summer home where he could make a little wine in the basement like his grandparents once did'), and over thirty years since 1975 he has restored the Inglenook Château and grounds and invested heavily in a new winery, underground cellars and in organic certification of the 80 hectares of vineyards.

Much of the land was bought with the profits of his film of *Dracula*, with *The Godfather: Part III* chipping in as well. For Coppola, 'It all goes back to the land. If you have the land, you have the grapes and if you have the grapes, you have the wine.' And his goal has always been 'to make one of America's great wines'. The price of the Rubicon line – $140 (£80) per bottle of the Cabernet Sauvignon red – suggests he is getting there. He reportedly paid over $350,000 (£200,000) per acre for the neighbouring land, a record price for an American vineyard. The wines from this estate would need to retail at over £75 per bottle to justify this price.

SKYWALKER WINE

Coppola is not averse to exploiting his film-making background. With George Lucas (his collaborator on *American Graffiti*) he produces a $30 (£17) Chardonnay named Viandante del Cielo ('Skywalker' in Italian). The grapes are grown at Lucas's Skywalker ranch and vinified at Coppola's winery. The 2002 bottling was the first commercial release, though Coppola and Lucas have been making wine together since 1990.

GÉRARD DEPARDIEU – *VIGNERON*

Actor Depardieu, whose passport describes him as *vigneron* (a wine-grower), has properties in the Loire Valley (the Château de Tigné), the Languedoc and Bordeaux. In Jonathan Nossiter's unexpected hit documentary of 2004, *Mondovino*, a final twist concerns Depardieu. The film is centred on the efforts of Robert Mondavi Wine to acquire a property at Aniane in the Languedoc. Finally, thanks to the ferocious opposition of local growers and the communist mayor, the bid is beaten off. It then transpires that the land has been sold to Depardieu and his millionaire partner, Bernard Magrez, at a price of £26,000 per hectare – far more than the locals can afford. 'Mondavi, Depardieu . . . I can't see the difference!' is the conclusion of

Aniane's former mayor. A touch unfair, given the reputation that the wines of Château de Tigné have won from critics up to and including Robert Parker himself. Depardieu himself attributes his wine 'epiphany' to a bottle of Château Rayas 1955 that he was given to taste in 1968. He is now said to have the world's best collection of this wine from the Châteauneuf-du-Pape appellation.

WINE ON FILM

For a documentary, *Mondovino* was an unexpected hit. On a different scale – but equally surprising – was *Sideways*, directed by Alexander Payne and released in 2004 to acclaim and Oscar nominations. In *Sideways*, Miles (divorced schoolteacher with a taste for Pinot Noir) takes his old roommate Jack (a has-been actor) on a tour of the wineries and restaurants of Santa Ynez. The tour is to mark Jack's last taste of the bachelor life in the week before his marriage.

The film uses wine as a metaphor for deeper issues. When Miles describes what he loves in Pinot he is describing himself. It's 'a hard grape to grow [. . .] thin-skinned, temperamental . . . needs constant care and attention. It's not a survivor like Cabernet, which can just grow anywhere and thrive even when it's neglected. It can only really grow in these really specific, little tucked-away corners of the world. And only the most patient and nurturing of growers can really do it.' Miles would not be a fan of the current wave of American Pinots, often described as 'Pinot on steroids'.

Pinot sales in New York rose after the film was released and, overall, sales during the six months after release were up by over 20 per cent. Merlot sales declined. There has been vigorous debate in the USA since the film's release about whether or not Miles is an alcoholic, a 'problem drinker' or just a drinker who goes over the top every now and then. Pointing to the scene where he drinks from a spittoon, most commentators concluded he was well on the way to alcoholism. The actor who played Miles (Paul Giamatti) agreed his character did have a 'drink problem'.

CHAMPAGNE HUGH

In 1989, Hugh Grant starred in a made-for-TV movie of the life of the original 'Champagne Charlie', Charles-Camille Heidsieck, who opened up the US market for champagne in the mid-nineteenth century. Heidsieck created his own brand and by 1857 was selling 300,000 bottles a year in the USA – the fruit of four trips across the Atlantic earlier that decade. The 1989 picture is not highly rated, and even fan websites describe it as a 'yawn biopic'. The musical *Champagne Charlie*, written by George Leybourne, was a smash London hit in the late Victorian age. Alas for Heidsieck, it promoted Moët & Chandon with the lines:

> *Champagne Charlie was my name,*
> *Champagne drinking gain'd my fame,*
> *So as of old when on the spree,*
> *Moët and Chandon's the wine for me.*

Moët & Chandon on the Race Track

It has become traditional in Formula 1 Grand Prix racing for top-three-placed drivers to spray each other (and the crowd) with Moët & Chandon champagne from the podium. Moët started the practice of offering champagne to the winners in the 1930s. American driver Dan Gurney is credited with the modern practice of spraying the crowd with champagne after his victory in the Le Mans 24-hour race in 1967 with A. J. Foyt as co-driver. Moët became the official champagne from 1972 onwards until 2000, when Mumm took over.

Not every race has its share of champagne. There were no celebrations after the 1994 Italian Grand Prix in which Ayrton Senna died, and Michael Schumacher refused to celebrate his 2004 victory in the European Grand Prix as a mark of respect for Umberto Agnelli, the veteran Ferrari chairman, who had died earlier in the week.

Another exception from spraying champagne to signal victory is the USA's Indianapolis 500 racing spectacle. There the victor receives a quart bottle of chilled milk. The tradition was established in 1936 by Louis Meyer, a triple winner of the endurance event. There's no accounting for taste . . .

However, champagne celebrations have managed to survive official bans. At the 1997 French Grand Prix Bernie Ecclestone, F1's supremo, had to buy the champagne himself in defiance of the French government's ban on alcohol advertising.

Even those who rue the waste of good champagne accept that such exuberant use of the drink has done much to build the image of champagne as the wine of celebration.

MOST EXPENSIVE MEAL (PER HEAD)

Despite its reputation as the drink of the rich and famous, at one infamous celebration champagne was merely a bit-part player. Six London bankers celebrating a market coup dined in style at Pétrus, formerly Gordon Ramsay's flagship London restaurant. Their wine list read:

Wine	Price
Château Pétrus 1945	£11,600
Château Pétrus 1946	£9,400
Château Pétrus 1947	£12,300
Château d'Yquem 1900	£9,200
Château Le Montrachet 1982	£1,400
Total	£43,900

In addition to this, six glasses of champagne, two beers and a packet of cigarettes totalled £102. The restaurant chose to waive the cost of the actual food – £360. Five of the bankers were sacked within the week by their employer, Barclays Capital, despite the fact that they had paid with their own money. The bank was clearly sensitive to the PR impact of its employees making so much money from a deal – and a client.

MORGAN AT THE MIRABELLE

In his recent autobiography, *Inside Story*, Piers Morgan, former editor of UK tabloid the *Daily Mirror*, boasts about lunching with Marco Pierre White at the chef's Mirabelle restaurant, which is famed for its wine list. Dining at the latter's expense, the pair were celebrating White's forthcoming marriage and Morgan's travails over share-tipping allegations (of which he was later cleared). At one point, Morgan enquired about the price of the wine they had been drinking. White produced a printout showing a total of £260 for the food and £26,000 for the wine. The goodies that Marco Pierre White had supplied included:

Château Mouton-Rothschild 1945
Château d'Yquem 1911 (£11,000 for one bottle)
Two glasses of 1900 cognac.

White justified the Yquem on the grounds that 'I'm getting married and you've had a hard time and we're celebrating.' He signed the bottle for Morgan with the quip: '£1,500 a sip – love Marco.'

YQUEM FEAST

In her book *Food and Wine Adventures* Jancis Robinson MW describes a feast at Château d'Yquem held in 1986 by German collector Hardy Rodenstock. Amongst other rarities the forty guests tried an Yquem dated around 1750 that Rodenstock had discovered in Russia – probably a relic of the Tsar's cellars in Leningrad. The bottle was flask-shaped, made of 'deep indigo-coloured glass engraved all over, and with white-painted flowers, grapes and vine leaves.' The date of the wine was established only through analysis of the glass. Jancis Robinson MW describes the wine thus: 'deep foxy red, creamy rich in texture, almost unctuous with a slight minerally edge'. She felt that though it was starting to 'fall apart' it was still a naturally sweet wine of the highest quality.

AUCTION RECORDS

The largest wine auction in the world is the annual Napa Valley Wine Auction. The Napa Auctions have been running for over twenty years and during the 2004 event hit a landmark $50 million (£30 million) in total revenue. The 2000 auction remains the bestselling of all – raising over $9.5 million (£5.5 million). This auction also included the most expensive single lot ever auctioned for charity. This was a ten-year vertical (i.e. the same wine from ten consecutive vintages) of magnums of Harlan Estate Red Wine from 1987 to 1996 which sold for $700,000 (£400,000) to B. A. 'Red' Adams, an auction veteran from Louisiana. This is equivalent to $28,000 (£16,000) per bottle.

Prices of this magnitude are typically fuelled by the clashing wallets and egos of Silicon Valley billionaires. These dizzying totals in 2000 owed much to a single generous bidder, retired Silicon Valley executive Chase Bailey, who placed more than $1.7 million (£980,000) in winning bids, including $500,000 (£290,000) for a six-litre bottle of 1992 Screaming Eagle Cabernet Sauvignon – a world record for a single bottle.

A 2003 bid of $320,000 (£183,000) made a Texan couple instant vintners. They bought Lot No. 90, which gave them the right to produce 300 cases of their own Napa Valley Cabernet Sauvignon. The lot included everything from grapes and vinification to a marketing plan. Supplementary sponsorship raised the total value of the bid to $1 million (£570,000).

MONEY WINES

Outside of the charity-auction scene the records are rather more realistic, even if not exactly down to earth. Christie's raised $420,500 (£240,000) for a single lot of fifty cases of Mouton-Rothschild 1982 – over $7,000 (£4,000) a bottle. Indeed, 1982 was a great year for Bordeaux. Michael Broadbent gives it five stars and comments that it was Robert Parker's 'enthusiastic pronouncements' on 1982 that made his (i.e. Parker's) name.

The highest-priced single case was Mouton-Rothschild 1945 (another very great year) that went for just under $10,000 (£5,800) a bottle. A single case of Latour 1961 consigned to auction by François Pinault, the château's owner, made $56,400 (£33,000) at auction in Los Angeles in November 2004. The oldest of these great wines and still drinking 'impressively', according to Michael Broadbent, was a double magnum of Lafite-Rothschild 1865 which Christie's sold for £27,500 in July 2001.

A seven-bottle lot of Montrachet 1978 from Domaine de la Romanée-Conti made $167,500 (£96,000) – just under $24,000 (£14,000) per bottle – at Christie's in New York in 2001. This per-bottle price was beaten in October 2004 when a single bottle of Yquem reached $71,675 (£41,000) at a Zachy's auction in Los Angeles, making it the single most expensive bottle ever sold in the USA.

New World Records – The Grange Effect

Of New World wines, perhaps the most expensive was a single bottle of Penfolds Grange 1951, bought in June 2004 by Lance Vater, an Australian businessman intent on building up a full set of Grange from 1951 onwards. He paid US$50,200 (£28,000) and was doubtless relieved when Peter Gago, the Penfolds winemaker, pronounced it to be in fine condition at one of Penfolds regular re-corking clinics (see page 34). The 1951 was an experimental wine from the collection of Max Schubert, the creator of Grange. The final vertical tasting of the complete Grange range from 1951 onwards was held in late 2003. Stocks are now too low for further complete tastings.

A higher price was paid in 2003 for an impériale (six litres) of Grange shortly before its international release. An unidentified man, believed to be bidding for an overseas buyer, paid US$71,040 (£41,000).

A complete vertical of Penfolds Grange – from 1951 to 1991 – sold for $70,500 (£40,000) at the Zachy's inaugural Los Angeles auction in late 2004. This made it the most expensive Australian wine ever sold at auction in the USA. There are said to be fewer than sixty bottles left of the Grange 1952, which was the first year to be sold commercially. Its price then was roughly equivalent to $1 today. However, prices of Grange have generally dropped by around 35 per cent since the mid-1990s.

A single bottle of 2002 Torbreck Les Amis Grenache from the Barossa Valley was sold for $70,000 (£40,000) at the Naples Winter Wine Festival Charity Auction in 2004.

The top price paid for a bottle of white wine was $71,675 (£41,000) for an 1847 Château d'Yquem bought by Roman Coppola (Francis Ford Coppola's son) at a Los Angeles auction. Coppola also bought two bottles of the fabled 1941 Cabernet Sauvignon from the Inglenook Winery. He explained that they were part of his father's efforts to rebuild the library of wines related to properties he now owns (see page 78).

These wines were at least drinkable. The world's most expensive bottles were not.

THE WORLD'S MOST EXPENSIVE BOTTLES

James Christie's first ever sale in 1766 realized £175 for 'a large quantity of Madeira and high flavour'd claret'. Just over two hundred years later, a bottle of 1787 Château Lafite later fetched £105,000 at a Christie's sale in London. This was a good year – unlike 1788 and 1789, whose bad harvests contributed to the unrest leading up to the French Revolution. The rarity and the price were enhanced by the initials on the glass – 'Th. J.' – those of Thomas Jefferson, third President of the United States, and wine adviser to several of his successors. Jefferson knew his wine, and bought direct from vineyards in Burgundy and Bordeaux (even if *en primeur* hadn't yet been invented). Jefferson's initials were engraved on the bottle along with the name of the wine, which in the pre-label era proved ownership and provided identification of the wine.

The 1787 Lafite was bought for the Forbes Collection by billionaire collector Malcolm Forbes. Rumour has it that the cork dried out under the display-case lights and fell into the wine. Not that it would have been drinkable anyway.

Another of Jefferson's bottles was a 1787 Margaux – celebrated as the world's most expensive wine even though it was never sold. Advertised by wine merchant William Sokolin for $500,000 (£285,000) it was broken by a clumsy waiter. The insurers paid out $225,000 (£130,000), which was split between Sokolin and the owner of the wine.

THE THOMAS JEFFERSON EFFECT

Jefferson was also the original owner of the most expensive white wine ever sold – a 1787 Château d'Yquem. This was a great year for Yquem – though perhaps not quite the equal of the 1784, of which Jefferson bought 250 bottles. He also bought Château Margaux – both the 1784 and 1787 vintages. The price for the former was 'trois livres'. The Yquem library stocks still include one bottle of the 1787. Count Alexandre Lur-Saluces, the inspiration behind Yquem in the twentieth century, has some doubts about its claimed Jeffersonian provenance: 'There are rather a lot of them about,' he says.

Jefferson did order Sauternes for 'our President, General Washington'. He himself wanted ten dozen and ordered thirty dozen for George Washington, reporting to Louis-Amedée de Lur-Saluces (the first of that family to own

Yquem) that 'the white wine of Sauterne . . . was so well received by the Americans who tasted it that I do not doubt it will generally conform to the taste of my compatriots.' It was George Washington himself who said 'my manner of living is plain, a glass of wine and a bit of mutton are always ready, and such as will be content to partake of that are always welcome.'

Jefferson believed in the health-giving powers of wine. Commenting on a proposed tax on wines he said, 'I think it is a great error to consider a heavy tax on wines as a tax on luxury. On the contrary, it is a tax on the health of our citizens.' He did, however, spend 12 per cent of his annual salary on wine during his years in the White House. He was paid $25,000 a year (equivalent to $490,000/£280,000) in today's currency) and $3,000 ($56,000/£32,000 today) went on wine. His eleven servants received a total of $2,700 (£1,500) in wages between them.

GREATEST APPRECIATION

A case of 1982 Le Pin cost £185 at first offer. It is now worth £26,000. When Montana bought 1,200 hectares of land around Cloudy Bay in New Zealand in 1973, they paid just over NZ$1,100 (£430) per hectare. That land is now worth between NZ$60,000 and NZ$120,000 ((£24,000 and £48,000) per hectare. Although Montana used the name Cloudy Bay Company for the firm that bought the land they did not register the name. That would have produced a higher return on the investment. Their initial wine, produced in 1980, was the first Marlborough Sauvignon Blanc. Its pungent cut-grass flavours caused an international sensation.

To Spit or Not to Spit

Cloudy Bay was so named by its Australian founder, David Hohnen, after the colour of the bay, which is caused by silt from the Wairau River that turns it sandy coloured. The clouds on the label came later. But Cloudy Bay was not the first choice of name. Originally Hohnen considered naming the wine after another local feature. We could have been drinking – and admiring – Farewell Spit. Originally, Semillon was added in warm years but this is no longer done and winemaker Kevin Judd claims it's the 5 per cent barrel fermentation that gives the wine its 'subliminal dimension'.

Robert Parker and His Points

Robert Parker, now probably the most influential wine writer in the world (for better or worse), and his 'Parker points' did much for that Le Pin appreciation. He began to use a 100-point marking system for wines in the mid-1970s when he started the *Wine Advocate*.

Before that time, the 20-point system created by the University of California at Davis had largely ruled the wine-assessment market, and in particular, the commercial judging of wines.

Other wine writers (and other countries) use different systems. Michael Broadbent follows an old-established English tradition by using star ratings. Five stars is the best. His book on great vintages does, however, note that he gave at least two wines a higher rating than his five-star maximum: the Château Léoville of 1864 ('seven stars') and Château Lafite 1871 ('six stars'). The influential Italian guide *Gambero Rosso* uses only three points. These are expressed in the shapes not of stars but of glasses. So 'tre bicchieri' (three glasses) is a top wine.

The Parker system, which bears comparison with the American pupil-assessment range of 65 to 100 points, scores from 50 to 100 only. Fifty is undrinkable; 100 is perfection.

ABANDONED WINES

Until the beginning of 2003 Fortnum & Mason, the London store, offered free cellarage to valued customers. When they closed the cellars they still had numerous unclaimed cases of wine, including one of Château Latour 1949. The wine, rated at a perfect 100 points by Robert Parker, had been in the cellars since the 1970s. Estimated value of the Latour – £20,000.

THE PARKER EFFECT

Since the mid-1970s only some 127 wines have achieved the fabled (and immensely valuable) 100-Parker-point rating. As Robert Parker himself puts it, this is 'one-tenth of one per cent of the wines I've tasted.'

A lucrative mini-industry has sprung up to exploit the 100-pointers for commercial and charitable purposes. An American wine store sells as a 'perfect gift' a mixed case of Parker 100-pointers. The price is $10,000 (£5,800).

A 2004 tasting of ten 100-point wines led by Parker's colleague Pierre Rovani raised $150,000 (£86,000) from just a hundred tickets (naturally). The event – with associated auctions – raised over $300,000 (£170,000) for charity. Parker himself led a similar tasting to raise funds to endow the Robert Parker Wine Advocate Scholarships at the Culinary Institute of America. The cost per person for this event was $2,000 (£1,200) for twelve wines. In order of age the wines were:

1975 La Mission-Haut-Brion
1976 Penfolds Grange
1982 Château Pichon-Longueville Comtesse de Lalande
1986 Château Mouton-Rothschild
1990 Paul Jaboulet Aîné Hermitage La Chapelle
1991 Marcel Chapoutier Côte-Rôtie La Mordorée
1992 Dalla Valle Vineyards Maya Cabernet Sauvignon
1996 Château Lafite-Rothschild
1997 Screaming Eagle Cabernet Sauvignon, Napa Valley
2000 Château Margaux
2000 Château Pavie St-Emilion
2001 Harlan Estate

The port was Taylor's Fladgate 1992.

THE SCORING SYSTEM

The Parker scoring system runs from 50 to 100. The system criteria are:

Score	Characteristics
50–59	A wine deemed to be unacceptable.
60–69	A below-average wine containing noticeable deficiencies, such as excessive acidity and/or tannin, an absence of flavour, or possibly dirty aromas or flavours.
70–79	An average wine with little distinction except that it is soundly made. In essence, a straightforward, innocuous wine.
80–89	A barely-above-average to very good wine displaying various degrees of finesse and flavour as well as character with no noticeable flaws.

90–95   An outstanding wine of exceptional complexity and character. In short, these are terrific wines.

96–100   An extraordinary wine of profound and complex character displaying all the attributes expected of a classic wine of its variety. Wines of this calibre are worth a special effort to find, purchase and consume.

Critics would argue that because the system does not specifically deduct points for wines that are, for example, excessively cloudy, it is less precise than the UC Davis scores. Nor does it allow for distinguishing between the wines at the very top; hence British expert Serena Sutcliffe's facetious award of 101 points to the Billecart-Salmon, Cuvée Nicholas-François 1959 at the Millennium Champagne tasting in Sweden.

PARKER DECONSTRUCTED

One critic, John Dvorak, has gone so far as to 'reverse engineer' the system and come up with his own interpretation of the scores.

Parker Score	*Actual Characteristics*
100	No such thing. Theoretically impossible as far as I'm concerned. It means total perfection. Used by Parker to get attention and mock the industry.
95–99	Great wine that should be purchased under any circumstance. A fabulous product that an idiot could spot.
91–94	Not absolutely sure how good these wines really are but they could be great. The difference between 91 and 94 has nothing to do with the wine and everything to do with the confidence level of the taster. Unfortunately, over-confident 'greatest wine ever from this château' tasters such as James Suckling [*Wine Spectator*] always boost the number too far. Whatever the case, these wines are recommended. Parker is always more accurate in this range than *Wine Spectator*.

Parker Score	Actual Characteristics
90	This is the chickenshit ranking. It means the tasters are scared to rank this wine higher – they may be wrong. On the other hand they can't take a chance on ranking it as an 89 either. This rating really means: try it yourself and *you* be the judge.
86–89	Gosh, the wine is drinkable. It might be good. We may be wrong. Beyond that who knows?
81–85	You have to be real thirsty and hard up to drink from this group. The 85 rating means you can probably choke it down in a pinch.
75–80	Wouldn't want to even open a bottle!
Below 75	Can we be sued for saying what we really think?

PARKER, PAVIE AND PENIS WINES

Parker's preferences for wine style are not universally shared. He had a spat with Jancis Robinson MW over the 2003 release of wines from Château Pavie. She called his 96- to 100-point rating 'ridiculous'. One female sommelier is in the habit of referring to the super-extracted high-alcohol wines that Parker tends to rate most highly as 'penis wines'. James Halliday, perhaps the most eminent of all Australian judges of wine, has expressed his dislike of what he calls Parker's preferred 'battleship galactica' style. However, the Pavie was released at nearly $1,000 (£580) per case and it was sold by the eminent London merchants, Berry Bros & Rudd, at £83 per bottle. Controversy does not hurt ... even when it leads to legal action.

LEGAL ACTIONS

Wine is a litigious business. Most effort – and most money – is spent on protecting a name.

In 2001 Moët & Chandon sued Channon Wines of Queensland, Australia, for 'passing off'. The French won (they usually do) but the outcome was a PR and sales triumph for the tiny winery. They renamed their wines as Robert Channon Wines and achieved the best sales they had ever had.

The producers of champagne, as individual houses and via their trade body CIVC (Comité Interprofessionel du Vin de Champagne), are among the most litigious.

CHAMPAGNE VERSUS CHAMPAGNE

In 2004 a long legal battle forced the commune of Champagne in Switzerland to abandon the use of its name for local wines. The 670 villagers, who claim to have been making wine since Roman times, emphasized the differences. 'Our [wine] is flat, red or white, and practically only sold in Switzerland,' said the mayor. Furthermore, he claimed, the village's annual production of 280,000 bottles of red and white wine from local Chasselas grapes was only one-hundredth of that of the Champenois's 290 million bottles. To no avail. They lost the case.

The French have been less successful with the South American town of Garibaldi, which still advertises itself as the 'Champagne Capital of Brazil'. Their website invites the visitors to 'drink a cup of

champagne'. The website of the Embassy of Brazil proudly boasts non-alcoholic 'guarana champagne'.

There is, however, a new threat to the Champenois. The World Trade Organization (WTO) ruled in early 2005 that non-EU countries can use geographic descriptors such as 'champagne', seeing such limitations as protectionist. The EU, which has banned such usage to protect local producers, has announced it will appeal.

MORRISON VERSUS MORRISON

Musician Van Morrison sued British supermarket chain, Wm Morrison, for applying to register the name Vins Morrison. The supermarket was unrepentant, but the wine is no longer on their shelves.

Gallo Wines of California forced a businesswoman selling ceramic roosters (*gallo*, in Italian) under the names *gallo verde*, *gallo rosso* and *gallo blu* to switch to the word *galletti*. They were able to do so because Italian is not an official language in America. The descriptions have been used for centuries for ceramics from Deruta, the Italian town that specializes in majolica pieces.

THE TOKAY CASE

Another long-running battle was that over the word 'Tokay'. As part of the negotiations about Hungary's accession to the EU, it was agreed that both Tokay d'Alsace (a light, dry wine made from Pinot Gris) and Tocai Friulano (an aromatic Italian white made from the Tocai grape, known in France as Sauvignon Vert) would no longer be permitted to use the word 'Tokay' or 'Tocai'. The reason for this was that the Hungarians feared that Tokaji, their historic dessert wine which is exported under the Tokay name, might suffer. They have, however, reached an agreement with Slovakia which will allow that country's winemakers to produce Tokay from 560 hectares of historic Tokay *terroir* that now lies on the far side of the Hungarian border.

The Alsatians now use Tokay-Pinot Gris d'Alsace. That option is not open to the Italians because Tocai is the name of the grape. The ability to use Tokay as part of the Alsatian name will be withdrawn in 2006. The most recent appeals to the EU Advocate General were dismissed in late 2004. Nobody knows what will happen now, but neither the growers nor the Italian government are happy.

WHAT'S IN A NAME?

The French are resistant to the use of the name Shiraz (as distinct from Syrah) for wines produced in France. The name was therefore not originally recognized by the EU as a valid descriptor. J. Sainsbury plc, the UK supermarket chain, paid a high price for this. They were forced to take Wild Pig Shiraz, a Vin de Pays d'Oc, off their shelves and relabel the bottles. Sales then fell by 40 per cent. This mistake was not one that Le Piat d'Or made.

WHY THE FRENCH DO NOT ADORE LE PIAT D'OR

Le Piat d'Or is a creation of the English advertising industry. Launched in a test market in 1978, it became the UK's most popular wine brand within months of a new advertising campaign airing in 1984, and still remains one of the top dozen UK brands. The competition at that time was Paul Masson, Lutomer, Hirondelle and other such car-crash wines of the 1980s.

The ads started with a young French beauty introducing her irascible father to her English fiancé. He is not impressed until the fiancé produces a bottle or two of Piat d'Or. With that Papa melts and the commercial closes with family dinner and the immortal line: 'The French adore Le Piat d'Or'. It is rumoured that Piat d'Or was at that time a white wine with red colouring added. Recent research suggests that such a practice would have been a very effective technique to win over novice drinkers.

The French did not adore Le Piat d'Or because they were never given the chance to try it. They may not have been enthusiastic if they had. A *Which?* report of early 2005 reviewing the top brands of wine in the UK market ranked Le Piat d'Or bottom overall (though Banrock Station Merlot scored worse in the red category). This, it should be noted, after a relaunch of Piat d'Or in 2001 which stressed that it was now going to be a 'really decent mouthful of wine'. Glaswegian consumers appeared to agree in a Piat d'Or taste test carried out in 2003, which saw both red and white Piats outscore their medium-priced and higher-priced competition.

The brand now covers three ranges: the core red and white, a dual-varietal range with names such as Piat d'Or Merlot Shiraz (taking advantage of recent EU rule changes which allow the name Shiraz to be used instead of Syrah for French wines made from this grape) and a single-varietal range. The 2004 advertising campaign shows a picture of an open bottle with the words: 'They say you should let wine breathe. Okay, that's long enough.'

Piat d'Or is, however, nectar compared to some of the world's more popular wines.

THUNDERBIRD

Amongst the most despised and yet most consumed 'wines' of the world is Thunderbird. The quote marks above are intentional.

As one commentator observes, 'If you like to smell your hand after pumping gas, look no further than Thunderbird [. . .] This ghastly mixture of unknown chemicals . . . turns your lips and mouth black. A mysterious chemical reaction similar to disappearing-reappearing ink makes you look like you've been chewing on hearty lumps of charcoal.'

Thunderbird was the creation of E. J. Gallo. In the aftermath of Prohibition in the USA, Ernest Gallo and his brothers were determined to capture the nascent wine market. Ernest's desire then was to become the 'Campbell Soup Company of the wine industry'.

To this end he created several cheap, highly fortified (20 per cent alcohol) wines such as Thunderbird (and White Port) for sale in inner-city neighbourhoods. The radio ad. went like this:

What's the word? – Thunderbird.
How's it sold? – Good and cold.
What's the jive? – Bird's alive.
What's the price? – Thirty twice.

Gallo never truly shed its downmarket image despite creating more upmarket brands and despite donating huge sums to both the Republican and Democrat political parties. The donations had their effect, though. Senator Bob Dole (he of the Viagra ads) received $200,000 (£115,000) for supporting a tax amendment that helped the family gain inheritance-tax concessions. It is Gallo's greatest desire to see his grandchildren 'come into their winery', which is now the largest in the world. Do not forget that it is founded upon Thunderbird . . .

GARAGE WINES AND *GARAGISTES*

From one extreme of the world of made wines to the other. The name *vins de garage* was coined by Michael Bettane, the French wine consultant, to describe wines produced in Bordeaux in tiny quantities. The essence of garage wines is that they are formulated around tiny yields (between 12 and 40 hectolitres per hectare) of the finest grapes from mature vines. Meticulous care in the vineyard, ruthless pruning and multiple passes through the vineyard when harvesting (*tris*) ensure that only the best of the grapes survive to be picked at the optimum point of ripeness.

The first *garagiste* (a small-time winemaker) was probably Jean-Luc Thunevin of Château Valandraud. He was a bank employee before he set up his winery; his first commercial vintage was in 1991.

Such winemaking aims for maximum concentration and colour extraction whilst maintaining soft tannins. That means slow fermentation, lengthy skin contact and the pumping of oxygen into the must to accelerate its evolution. A minimum of 100 per cent new French oak is used. Many wines are subjected to 200-per-cent exposure with the wine being racked from one set of new barrels to another. Le Pin, Valandraud, Mondotte, Marajollia and others pull in high Parker points and even higher prices. Many wine writers feel that garage wines are a prime example of 'emperor's new clothes' syndrome and that time will reveal them to be overpriced wines made for gullible collectors. Canadian MW Michael Palij goes further, comparing Valandraud to Gallo: 'Each is a triumph of style

over substance. Neither pays any regard to either history or *terroir*.'
Not all would agree with this comparison.

Another Gallo connection is to Fred Franzia, Gallo's nephew and
creator of the famous (or infamous) Two-Buck Chuck.

TWO-BUCK CHUCK

A product of the Californian wine lake, Two-Buck Chuck sold
8 million cases in two years from launch in 2002. The formal name
of the wine is 'the Charles Shaw range' and it is produced by the
Bronco Wine Company, which is part of the Franzia wine-box
business. However, the Charles Shaw range comes in bottles rather
than boxes or jugs, which gives it a more exclusive feel. The actual
price range is from $1.99 to $3.50 per bottle, and it has fascinated
and exasperated Californian winemakers with higher ambitions and
higher prices by its sales success and by the extensive media
coverage it has received.

Much of the coverage has cast doubt on the wisdom of those who
drink more expensive products. According to most wine writers,
however, 'it sucks'. One tasting note referred to it as 'cranberry juice
spiked with rubbing alcohol'. However, at least one writer has
proclaimed it to be a revolution because it is a fully dry wine, unlike
the box wines which are almost all off-dry thanks to added sugar.

Urban myth has it that the wine was a by-product of the post-9/11
airline scare. Corkscrews were banned on aircraft and the wine
was bought from American Airlines for a song. Fred Franzia's
explanation for his success is production on a mass scale. Bronco has
vineyards where the tractors drive for 3 miles before reaching the end
of a row and where 3,000 tons of grapes are moved every night.

Bronco's wines include several with the word 'Napa' in the brand
name. The US courts have ruled that such wines must contain
grapes from Napa. Bronco is currently appealing this to the US
Supreme Court.

AMERICA BOYCOTTS THE FRENCH – ROUND 1

It took many years of sustained pressure for the Americans even partly to abandon the practice of using European names such as Chablis. The Americans, like the Australians, view the French as their number-one value and volume benchmark. The persistent, if sometimes latent, American hostility to the 'cheese-loving surrender monkeys' has resulted in a number of boycotts of French wine. The current Iraq war was not the first time the Americans attempted to take their revenge on French wine producers.

After General Charles de Gaulle had made some provocative statements about the USA, New York wine merchants decided on a conspicuous gesture to the French president. French wine bottles were shown being smashed on TV and great wines were sold off at bargain prices. Charles Aznavour, the French singer–songwriter, was one grateful beneficiary of that boycott. He was able to buy a whole series of top wines for 99 cents a bottle, perhaps a tenth of their real value.

AMERICA BOYCOTTS THE FRENCH – ROUND 2

Evidence suggests that on another occasion when the Americans grew tired of the French during the run-up to the most recent Iraq war, merchants at least were a touch more canny. In 2003 restaurateurs in various states declared boycotts of French wine and replaced them with Californian, Oregon and Australian products; right-wing talk-show host Bill O'Reilly urged Americans to quit buying French products; a Pennsylvanian state representative called for legislation to ban French wine from the States; and a convenience-store owner set-up 'Do Not Cross' hazard-tape warnings in front of the French wine section of his store. However, as one store owner put it, the French wine was already in the country. The boycott was hurting no one but the importers. Others reportedly went out of their way to 'buy French wine and lots of other French stuff, just to piss off the Republicans.'

In such places as the House of Representatives canteen and aboard *Air Force One*, 'French fries' and 'French toast' were renamed 'freedom fries' and 'freedom toast'. Wine sales were, however, more affected by Robert Parker's refusal to cross the Atlantic for the *en primeur* tastings.

CONSTITUTIONAL CELEBRATIONS

Along with their dislike of the French, the Americans have always had an ambivalent attitude to alcohol. The Fathers of the American Constitution were, like the first settlers, fond of alcohol. The celebration party for the fifty-five drafters of the Constitution included fifty-four bottles of Madeira (the favourite drink of the time), sixty bottles of claret, eight bottles of whiskey, twenty-two bottles of port, eight bottles of hard cider, twelve beers and seven bowls of alcohol punch. It was reported that the punchbowls were large enough for ducks to swim in.

This did not prevent persistent anti-alcohol campaigning that culminated in the excesses of the Prohibition era. This saw per capita consumption of alcohol increase massively in the thirteen years from 1920 when the country was officially dry.

PROHIBITION – THAT 'NOBLE EXPERIMENT'

From January 1920 to December 1933, America was subject to the Volstead Act, which prohibited the making, selling, importing or exporting of alcoholic beverages. The immediate effect was the shutting-down of many wineries; the longer-term impact was to encourage far greater consumption of alcohol throughout the USA. Scotch whisky and Irish whiskey sales increased enormously with supplies coming in from Jamaica and Canada. Speakeasies – liquor stores or clubs where illegal alcohol was served – flourished. In the mid-1920s the New York Police Commissioner noted that the number of drinking establishments had at least doubled during the period of Prohibition. It was at this time that the habit of drinking cocktails entered mainstream American life – the flavourings were essential to disguise the raw spirit produced in illicit stills.

GRAPE BRICKS – DO NOT ADD YEAST

Wine did not flourish during this period to the same extent as hard liquor, though Communion wine and tonic wine were profitable exceptions (see below). Production of wine was harder to conceal, but many wineries did a flourishing trade in selling 'table grapes' that were vinified at home. Wine had a lower unit value per bottle than whisky and lacked the latter's appeal to smugglers. But wine was still there for the asking. During the period of Prohibition a product called the 'Grape Brick' was sold. This was a block of dried and pressed grape concentrate with a packet of yeast attached. The instructions were clear: 'Do not add yeast or fermentation will result.' They were typically ignored.

MEDICINE MEN IN THE BATHROOM

Charles MacLean's *MacLean's Miscellany of Whisky* quotes extensively from an article written by Francis Redfern for the trade magazine of the Distillers Company. Redfern noted how, during Prohibition, hotel rooms featured signs requesting patrons to 'open their medicine in the bathroom'. In the bathroom there would be a bottle opener and a corkscrew chained to the wall.

Redfern observed of this period that 'hotel keepers soon found themselves compelled to defend themselves in this way after the "dry" law was enacted, as guests were known to wreck whole suites of bedroom furniture in desperate efforts to remove a [bottle] closure.' His ship for the voyage home – 'the largest in the world, owned by the US Government' – was supposedly totally 'dry' for the entire voyage but 'you could have filled the swimming bath . . . with the champagne and other liquors which were supplied openly to the passengers by the "wine steward".'

THERAPEUTIC WINES

One – legal – exemption during this time was wine taken 'for medicinal purposes', which was sold in drugstores. The laxity of the rules allowed for substantial consumption of tonic or 'therapeutic' wines; so much so that the American government was forced to act. They required makers of such wines to add an ingredient that would induce vomiting above a certain dosage level.

COMMUNION WINES

It was also legal to consume Communion wine during the period of Prohibition. From 1919 to 1931, Catholic priests had to be authorized by the Federal authorities to buy wine. The story that participants at the Eucharist were obliged to prove they were of Irish or Italian stock appears to be a myth. Numerous purportedly Christian sects sprang up and, with Federal permission, showed themselves keen consumers of Communion wine.

However, the Church itself was ambivalent about Communion wine. A number of theologians took the view that the Greek and Hebrew words meaning wine had in fact been mistranslated. They argued that the correct translation was 'grape juice', and an American dentist called Thomas Bramwell Welch developed a method of mass-producing grape juice for the Communion service.

COMMUNION WINE AND THE AMERICAN STATE

It is almost certainly illegal for prisoners in the US correction system to partake of Communion wine, even though Amerindian prisoners are allowed, under certain circumstances, to use peyote (which contains mescaline) in religious ceremonies in jail. To count as an Amerindian you need to have 25 per cent Native American blood.

The state of Florida revoked the probation order on a recovering alcoholic receiving counselling for DUI (driving under the influence) when he mentioned that he had participated in Communion services. His driving privileges were revoked for a further five years.

OENOLOGY AND THEOLOGY – SOME QUESTIONS

The Christian sacrament of Holy Communion celebrates the last supper of Jesus with His disciples. The usual practice is for each participant in the Eucharist to take a sip from a cup of wine that the celebrant has blessed.

This simple ceremony has attracted much scholarly and polemical debate over the centuries. Does the wine have to be fermented or is unfermented grape juice acceptable? Well, to some Christian groups unfermented grape juice is acceptable, but the orthodox view is that it must be fermented. Should it be mixed with water, as the ancient Jewish practice was? Should it be red (as is usual), or white? It can be either. Is sparkling wine acceptable? The answer, it would seem, is 'no', if the wine has been produced with the addition of carbon dioxide. This is because impure wines (i.e. those with chemical or other additives) are forbidden. So, in theory, *méthode traditionelle* wines should be acceptable. There is no record of such wines being used. Do celebrants have to consume all the consecrated wine? Yes, the blessed liquid may not be poured back into the bottle.

Lengthy studies have been conducted to determine whether or not the practice of sharing wine direct from the cup leads to increased risk of disease. The most recent study (by American microbiologist Anne LaGrange Loving in 1998) states emphatically that there is no increase in risk even though microbes are transferred during Holy Communion. The practice of intinction, in which the wafers are dipped in the wine by the celebrant, is no less susceptible to microbial transfer. She took a sample of 681 New Jersey individuals and found there were no differences in illness rates – regardless of whether wine was taken at Communion.

Little or no account is taken in such studies of the quality of the wine. According to pioneering Australian wine writer Walter James, such wines are typically stronger in theology than oenology. Wine has had a long theological and ecclesiastical career, though, and there are several contenders for the title of patron saint of wine and winemakers.

The Patron Saint of Wine

In approximate date order the candidates are: St Lawrence (died AD 258); St Vincent (died AD 304); St Martin (died AD 397); St Amand (died AD 679).

Done to a Turn

St Lawrence is primarily known as the patron saint of *rôtisseurs* on the grounds that he was executed by being grilled to death. Apparently he told his torturers, 'Turn me over, for I am cooked on this side.' He is patron saint of many different causes and professions

– including archivists, comedians (was that really his best joke?), paupers, glass-workers, vine-growers and winemakers. And of Sri Lanka. His feast day, on 10 August, is celebrated by a meal of cold meats.

HEAVEN'S WINEMAN

St Vincent was one of the early saints – unlike St Lawrence, who was canonized only in 1881. St Vincent was adopted as the patron saint of winemakers and vineyard workers in early medieval Europe. It is suggested that this is because the growers of the vines identified with his tortures as they struggled against mildew, frosts, drought, flood and insects. His legend is commemorated in vineyards and in wines. At La Mission in Bordeaux, there is a stone statue that is supposed to represent St Vincent himself turned into stone by an angry God. The story goes that Vincent was sent down to earth to visit the vineyards of France because God was so dissatisfied with the lack of good wine in Heaven. The wine at La Mission so entranced him that he forgot to return to Heaven – hence his stony punishment. An American vineyard produces a blend of Zinfandel and Sangiovese named in his honour.

THE INVENTOR OF PRUNING

St Martin was another of the early saints. He was a junior officer in the Roman army and became Bishop of Tours in AD 317 following many years as a hermit. He followed the Roman military custom of planting vines wherever he could and a number of legends point to his affinity with vine-growing. For example, his donkey once ate the vines to which it was tethered and Martin had to pay compensation to the enraged *vigneron*. When he returned a year later the grower was entranced by the quality of the crop. St Martin (or rather his donkey) had invented pruning. Despite this affinity, however, St Martin has become the patron saint of drunkards. St Martin's Day, 11 November, was regarded in many parts of Europe as the first day of winter. It was also an occasion for feasting and drinking the new wine. In parts of Germany, children would place jugs of water outside their doors in the expectation that the water would be magically transformed into wine. In the morning they would find – if they were lucky – that the water was indeed wine. A horseshoe-shaped pastry would be left beside the jug as a further sign that St Martin had passed that way during the night.

BREAD, WATER . . . AND WINE

St Amand was a Belgian missionary and hermit of the seventh century AD who evangelized the wine regions of northern Europe for many years. His patronage is narrow but deep: bar staff, bar keepers, brewers, hotel and innkeepers, merchants, vine-growers, vintners and wine merchants. The reason for these associations appears to be simply that he spent so much time preaching in wine-growing and brewing areas. His personal predilection for bread and water – on which he lived for fifteen years – is not held against him.

MICHAEL BROADBENT MW

No book about wine can be complete without an account of the life and times of Michael Broadbent, whom some would perhaps nominate as the modern patron saint of wine drinkers. (An alternative – for UK wine enthusiasts – might be Jancis Robinson MW, though she is more frequently referred to as 'HRH Jancis'. This does not in any way reflect her attitude to those around her but her stellar status among both the general populace and the 'cork dorks', as her friend and collaborator Tim Atkin MW refers to members of the trade.)

Michael Broadbent has been in the wine trade for fifty years; he knows (or appears to know) everyone of consequence; he was one of the first to pass the Master of Wine exams and has written two of the classics of twentieth-century wine-writing – *Wine Tasting* and *Michael Broadbent's Vintage Wines: Fifty Years of Tasting Three Centuries of Wine*, which celebrated its third edition in 2002.

Trained as an architect, Broadbent abandoned drainage pipes for wine in 1947 after tasting Yquem and Lafite. After working for a

London wine merchant and for Harvey's of Bristol he persuaded Christie's to take him on as head of their soon-to-restart wine auctions in 1965. This gave him licence to fossick to extraordinary effect in a large number of uncharted wine cellars around rural Britain and France, and in doing so amass the remarkable set of notes on great vintages that make up his *Vintage Wines*. His list of achievements and honours is lengthy, his columns in *Decanter* magazine unmissable and his enjoyment of life legendary.

From his experiences, he distilled for *Decanter* magazine in 2002 his list of the 'Ten Most Important Things I Have Learned'. They are:

* People are more important than organizations.
* Visit as many wine regions as possible – better a fleeting visit than none at all. It acts as an aide-memoire.
* Drink good wine with every meal. Half a bottle of good wine is more interesting – and better for you – than six bottles of plonk.
* Spot opportunities and have the courage to act on them.
* Start a tasting book and make notes.
* If you do not know the answer to a question, admit it.
* In wine, understanding is superior to pedantic knowledge.
* Read the classics on wine *and* keep up to date.
* Be honest and rely on your own tasting; avoid the influence of others.
* Teaching is the best way to learn.

MASTERS OF WINE

Broadbent was Chairman of the Institute of Masters of Wine in 1970. In this capacity he sat at the top of the wine world – if you discount those who actually own and make the stuff. At the time of

writing there are 246 Masters of Wine (though the number is increasing steadily) and 112 Master Sommeliers.

The first Master of Wine exams were held in 1953. Only six of the twenty-one candidates passed, and none of these original members are still living. Membership of the Institute of Masters of Wine was restricted for more than thirty years to British nationals but has been open to all comers since the mid-1980s, and there are now members of eighteen different nationalities. The first seventy-two members were all men and by 1979 there were still only three women. Now there are fifty-three. The highest day rate for a consultation is reputed to be that charged by Jancis Robinson MW, who took and passed the exam when five months pregnant.

The Master of Wine examination demands a sound grasp of that very English skill, essay writing, but the toughest part (for most candidates) is the tasting paper. Tim Atkin MW revealed in the *Observer* newspaper in 2004 that his training regime for the tasting exam consisted of a daily blind tasting of a dozen wines – for an entire year. Well over two thousand people have sat the exam but no more than one in ten makes it through.

Three men are both Masters of Wine and Master Sommeliers. One is Gerard Basset MW, who founded the Hotel du Vin chain in the UK. The other two are Doug Frost and Ronn Weigand, both American.

WINE JOBS – SOMMELIER

Being a sommelier is – if you are lucky – a way to explore and enjoy great wine every day and be paid a pittance. Wine jobs don't pay well – unless you're at the very top.

On average, British sommeliers do slightly better than their US counterparts, provided they are working in London – but neither can expect much in the way of reward, while French sommeliers may do better on tips.

Salary	UK (London) (£)	USA (£)	France (£)
On starting	14,000	8,000	10,000
Top of the range	35,000	23,000	34,000

For these salaries a lot is expected. Lettie Teague, Wine Editor of US magazine *Food & Wine*, spent three nights working as a sommelier at New York's Veritas restaurant, which has a list of over 3,000 labels. She concluded that a successful sommelier needed 'the stamina of a marathoner, the tact of a diplomat and the callused feet of a door-to-door salesman.'

The Wine Director (a term increasingly preferred in American restaurants to 'sommelier') at Veritas, Tim Kopec, has three criteria for would-be sommeliers. First is 'a strong back' – necessary when you are required to carry as many as 160 cases a day down to the cellar and bring back around 48 bottles in the evening. The second is computer skills, which is one reason why the ideal candidate should be in their mid-twenties. The third is a good palate and a clean palate (which entails no toothbrushing, no mints and no mouthwash after 3 p.m.).

Teague's conclusions: 'Sommeliers are the fighter pilots of the food world, making lightning-fast decisions under enormous duress. They keep mental notes on thousands of bottles, run upstairs and downstairs a hundred times a night and never get tired.'

An English equivalent, Matt Day, documented a rather more personal experience. He had to deal with a Texan who wanted 'no

Chardonahay' but requested a Premier Cru Chablis, and then declared the wine was corked. Day solved the problem by blaming the glass washer and offering a fresh glass. This was accepted and declared 'mighty fine'. He advised City bankers on which magnum of Pétrus (1966 or 1970) would go best with their dessert. He concluded his *Decanter* article by saying, 'give the sommelier a choice and he may well take you one step closer to food and wine heaven.'

THE WORLD'S LARGEST WINE LIST

The world's largest wine list is at Bern's Steak House in Florida. The 'working' cellar has one case of each of the 6,500 or so labels they stock but that only represents some 20 per cent of their total stock of around half a million bottles. This makes for a 2,500-page wine list, and ten wine waiters are on hand to help diners work out their preference. The list includes a 1792 Madeira (the oldest wine), two hundred wines by the glass and at least one wine with a price of over $10,000 (£5,800; a Gruaud-Larose 1851). Cellar tours are available but this is a functional area without the 'bordello-like' décor of the upstairs dessert rooms, which are fitted with television monitors for guests who can't bear to miss out on the football or the funnies.

THE PRICE OF THE LIQUID – RESTAURANTS

It is commonly accepted that drinkers subsidise non-drinkers in restaurants. The average mark-up on wine is three or four times (plus VAT). This is charged on the price the restaurant pays and, generally speaking, the more exclusive the restaurant the greater the mark-up. Other, fairer systems are a flat rate of a £10 mark-up (in the UK) for more expensive wines, or a sliding scale that reduces the mark-up as the base price increases.

The second-cheapest wine on the list is the one to avoid. Often it's the cheapest in terms of wholesale price. Nobody wants to look like a cheapskate, so nobody buys the cheapest wine on the list and no. 2 on the list is often the biggest seller – up to 50 per cent of the total volume of wine sold. Ask for the house wine instead.

Alternative strategies for choosing a wine include delegating the choice to any self-proclaimed expert in your party, or indicating your price range and preferred style to the sommelier and asking for their recommendation. But don't ask if the wine is good; ask whether they have tasted it and if so what it tastes like. If the answer is 'fruity' or 'generous' or 'full-bodied' then the odds are that the individual in question knows nothing. Do not take the advice. However, all is not lost . . .

THERE IS SUCH A THING AS FREE WINE

Felix Dennis, the UK magazine publisher who has made a fortune on both sides of the Atlantic from magazine gems such as *Maxim* and *Stuff*, hosts a poetry-reading tour called 'Did I Mention the Free Wine?' The ex-hippy, a defendant in the notorious *Oz* obscenity trial in the 1970s, turned poet after an illness in the late 1990s. To promote his book of poems, *A Glass Half Empty*, he put $600,000 (£340,000) of his own money into a poetry-reading tour of the USA. The draw was free wine. And it was not bad stuff. Premier Cru Chablis, Guigal Condrieu, Stags' Leap Chardonnay and Grand Cru Burgundy were among the featured wines. The price range was $25 to $100 (£14 to £57) a bottle and the plan was to serve over 10,000 glasses between the fourteen venues.

His verse has been compared with Kipling's, not so much for its quality as for its dogged rhyming structure. A sample:

> *Stands the glass half empty,*
> *Or stands the glass half full?*
> *Hand me the decanter, man.*
> *I'll take another pull.*

THE PRICE OF THE LIQUID – RETAIL

If you're buying on your own account from a retailer then a different and more complex set of calculations is required to arrive at the price of the liquid in your bottle. These calculations are valid for the United Kingdom only and are courtesy of Michael Palij MW.

Shop price	£2.99	£9.99
less VAT at 17.5%	£2.54	£8.50
less Retailer margin of 25%	£1.94	£6.50
less Duty	£0.68	£5.24
less Producer's margin of 20%	£0.57	£4.36
less 10p to cover corking/labelling etc	£0.47	£4.26

THE WINE OF THE WHITE HORSE

Although these price levels and pricing policies put a serious squeeze on the supply chain, producers have their little ways too. Christopher Fielden in Tom Stevenson's 2005 *Wine Report* refers to the Chilean practice of diluting the over-alcoholic must of Zinfandel or Syrah with water to enable it to ferment. Spotting a barrel with the letters 'CB' on it the visitor enquired what was within. *Caballo blanco* was the answer – water. This is illegal but not illogical since 500 litres of water added to 1,000 litres of must gives 50 per cent more wine. Fielden suggests the practice is also common in California.

ANIMALISTIC WINES

Caballo blanco – 'white horse' – is not the only animal in the wine trade. Coopers Creek vineyards in New Zealand have cornered the 'cat' market. Starting with Fat Cat Chardonnay and Cat's Pee on a Gooseberry Bush (Sauvignon Blanc), they have moved on to Tom Cat Merlot and Glamour Puss Pinot Noir. Cat's Pee is described by the makers as 'youthful, kittenish and extremely playful . . . equally happy relaxing on its own or engaging in boisterous antics with fresh seafood.' The ATF was unhappy with 'pee', so it is now 'Cat's Phee'. For every bottle sold in New Zealand a donation goes to the NZSPCA – further support for the cat cause.

Vampire Vineyards is, along with its sister brand Cupid Wines, a product of the post-Communism Romanian wine industry. The wines, which promise the 'taste of immortality', are basic varietals (Cabernet Sauvignon, Chardonnay, Pinot Noir and Pinot Grigio) aimed at the American market. A tasting kit of four bottles sells for $65 (£37) in the USA.

Then there is Fat Bastard. There are several stories about the origin of Fat Bastard. The label boasts a rather grumpy hippo and story number one suggests that the hippo was the eponymous Fat Bastard. The second was that the 'bastard' was a corruption of Bâtard-Montrachet. The true story appears to be that 'Thierry' (French winemaker Thierry Boudinaud) was newly back from Australia and keen to show off his recently acquired command of English slang to his friend Guy Anderson. That wine, he said, pointing to a particular barrel, 'eess a phet bastard'. And so the name was born – it was a Tuesday, says the website. Now it's the name of the winery and covers a range of wines from Chardonnay to Syrah.

THE FIRST BASTARD WINE

It was not, however, the world's first bastard wine. In the late fourteenth century the Portuguese were exporting *bastardo*. It is possible that this was a varietal, since the name Bastard is still given to one of the (many) port grapes, but it is more likely that it was a downmarket blend of honey and wine. Prince Hal in Shakespeare's *Henry IV Part 1* mocks a serving boy's come-on line, 'Score a pint of bastard in the Half-Moon,' and later tells him that 'your brown bastard is your only drink.'

Bastardo the grape has many synonyms – none of them very distinguished. In the Jura it's Trousseau; in the Lot it's Malvoisie Noir; in Argentina, Pinot Gris de Negro; and in California, Grey Riesling. It gives a full-bodied wine with sweet aromas – which some compare to dates. The Italian red wine Nerello del Bastardo has nothing to do with the grape Bastardo, however, being made from Nebbiolo and a touch of Sangiovese. Because it's an illegitimate blend (by the tenets of Italian wine laws) it can only be classified as a *vino da tavola*, the lowest grade. The name seeks to draw attention to this status by its reference to illegitimacy.

The goat market, by contrast, is South African owned. Charles Back's Fairview Estate has a range of wines with names that pun on Côtes du Rhône – despite the threats of legal action from the French authorities. First was Goats Do Roam, then came Goat Roti. Back claims that 'any similarities are purely incidental'. He also owns prize-winning herds of goats. When it comes to grapes, his philosophy is 'only [to] choose the bunches that you'd eat yourself,' which goes a long way towards justifying the cheek and the hype.

THE PRICE OF VINEYARD LAND

One piece of evidence that suggests that producers cannot be cast solely in the role of sufferers is the price of vineyard land. Tabulating the average price for such land is fraught with difficulty. Land quality varies, distance from the perceived centre of a wine-growing area reduces the price and, in any event, prices are subject to annual variation. If the land is bare the cost of development and planting will add another 80 to 100 per cent to the land cost. Here are some estimates of average prices for prime land.

Area	Average price
Napa Valley	$70,000 per acre
Oregon	$24,000 per acre
New Zealand	US$40,000 per acre
Central Otago, New Zealand	US$300,000 per ha
Marlborough	US$60,000 per ha
Tuscany (top areas)	US$2,000,000–3,000,000 per ha
Côtes de Provence	€30,000–60,000 per ha
Sancerre	€150,000 per ha
Beaujolais (Crus)	€45,000–115,000 per ha
Languedoc	€50,000 per ha
Alsace	€150,000 per ha
Châteauneuf-du-Pape	€300,000 per ha
Beaujolais (villages)	€20,000–45,000 per ha
Bordeaux (Graves)	€40,000–90,000 per ha
Bordeaux (St-Emilion, Pomerol)	€250,000–1,500,000 per ha
Champagne	£250,000 per acre
Kent (chalk soil)	£2,500 per acre

Francis Ford Coppola paid around $350,000 (£200,000) per acre for the Cohn Vineyard in Napa Valley in 2003. He outbid Robert Mondavi for this piece of prime Cabernet Sauvignon territory. It cost him $31.5 million (£18 million) against an initial asking price of $25 million (£14 million).

EXTREME VITICULTURE

Global warming along with improved techniques for growing vines and producing grapes are opening up new land all the time. Currently the most southerly vineyard in the world is Te Anau, on the route to Milford Sound in the South Island of New Zealand. The vineyard lies at 45° 25' South. Its grapes are not, however, processed on the premises, and the most southerly winery is at Black Ridge in Alexandra, south of Roxburgh in the South Island.

The most northerly vineyard is probably the Hallingstad Vineyard in Norway, which was established in 1995 by Sveier Hansen. It lies on a latitude of 60° North. Winemaking is only possible because of the influence of the nearby Oslofjord. The bulk of the wine is Pinot Noir (though there is some Riesling and Chardonnay). Each vintage of their Pinot Noir is bottled with a label showing one of Edvard Munch's paintings and, like Mouton-Rothschild's, there is considerable value in a complete series. The set of 'L'Esprit d'Edvard Munch' 1995–8 has nearly doubled in value in five years.

The Halfpenny Green Vineyard in the West Midlands of England (between Wolverhampton and Dudley) claims to be the 'most northern commercial red wine in the world'. Profits are £100,000 on a turnover of £800,000. Most of the profit comes not from the wine – whose quality is best described as mixed – but from a range of other commercial enterprises. As the owner says, 'If we had put some vines in a field and tried to sell the resulting wine we would have gone under.'

EQUATORIAL ESSENCES

In the middle, there is a vineyard on the equator in Uganda, though it produces grapes purely for personal use. The wines are reputed to be rather 'foxy'; that is, showing the effects of the *vitis labrusca* grapes rather than the classic *vitis vinifera*, and the vines are probably French hybrids brought over by French missionaries to make Communion wine. Uniquely, the climatic pattern of two dry seasons and two wet seasons makes it possible to produce two crops (and hence two vintages) per year.

HIGHEST VINEYARD

The highest commercial vineyard is probably that of Terror Creek in Western Colorado. It is 6,417 feet above sea level and is probably the only vineyard in the world whose wire fencing is required to keep out brown bears, mountain lions and lynxes, as well as raccoons. The temperature range is from 11°C (winter average) to 29°C (summer average), though the extremes are a lot more extreme. Production is currently around 700 cases per year and focused on Riesling and Gewürztraminer, though Pinot Noir, Gamay and Chardonnay have also been made.

A non-commercial vineyard in Bhutan (a landlocked nation in the Himalayas) is said to be situated above 7,200 feet. The highest in Europe is probably at Valdigne, near Mont Blanc. The vineyards are around 4,000 feet above sea level and produce low-alcohol table wines, including the evocatively named 'Blanc des Glaciers', as well as sparkling wines. Only one grape, the Blanc de Morgex, is grown, which has successfully adapted to the local climate. It has a delayed germination period and a rapid ripening phase. There may be vineyards as high or higher on Mount Etna where the temperate zone extends to around 4,250 feet above sea level.

SMALLEST VINEYARD

The world's smallest vineyard is believed to be the Africus Rex patio vineyard near Toronto. The vineyard is 7 foot by 11 foot square and is planted with Cabernet Franc bonsai vines. The grapes are grown with a hydroponic system (one in which no soil is needed), and the wine is vinified in the owner's cellar. The entire winery and cellar space is 108 square feet. Bonsai vines can be bought for around US$100 (£58) each and are 12 to 14 inches high. Varieties include Chardonnay, Zinfandel, Cabernet Franc and Cabernet Sauvignon.

THE PRISON VINEYARD

Prisoners at the Velletri jail south of Rome produce 45,000 bottles of wine a year. Their three wines (two red and one white) are labelled Fuggiasco ('Fugitive'), Quarto di Luna (a Chardonnay) and Sette Mandate ('Seven Turns of the Key'). Fuggiasco is a Novello wine – similar to Beaujolais Nouveau. It is advertised on the website of the Italian Ministry of Justice, which supported its production to the tune of nearly €500,000 (£350,000).

CLIMATE CHANGE

Global warming is a reality as far as the wine industry is concerned. In England, the ripening time for Reichensteiner grapes has advanced about three weeks over the last ten to fifteen years. If the Gulf Stream were to slow down then all wine production in the UK would cease, but most predictions suggest this is unlikely. The majority of scientists conclude that temperatures in the UK are likely to rise steadily over the next fifty years with the consequence that wine production would not only reach North Yorkshire – the northern limit of medieval cultivation – but stretch on into Scotland. In the shorter term, investment in the 'champagne' land of Kent could be a very good bet at one-hundredth of the price of equivalent land in France. Red wines would certainly benefit – with Pinot Noir and Dornfelder the key candidates for future success.

Harvest Dates

The summer of 2003 was one of exceptional heat. It produced some of the earliest harvest dates ever known across Europe and North America. *Nature* reviewed harvest dates for the Burgundian region since 1370 and concluded that 2003 was both the hottest summer and the earliest harvest date ever known. Other extraordinary years in more recent times include 1947 and 1893.

Harvest dates, of course, vary enormously by grape type. Both the earliest and the latest harvest dates for wines in the northern hemisphere are found in Sicily. There, Chardonnay grapes, transplanted to the southern coast at Menfi, are harvested in the last week of July. On the other side of the island, on the slopes of Mount Etna, Nerello Mascalese (a fashion grape of the future) is harvested in the last week of November. (These dates, of course, refer only to grapes that are not deliberately left on the vines to rot or sweeten.)

The American study that revealed the exceptional nature of 2003 also showed that, at least for the time being, global warming was benefiting the wine industry. The study showed an average temperature rise of 1.5°C and correlated this with higher vintage ratings on the 100-point scale used by auction house Sotheby's. A 1°C rise in temperature produced a 1.3-point increase in wine quality, with colder areas such as the Mosel and Rhine Valleys of Germany doing best from the warming climate. The authors of the study warn that a predicted further rise of 2°C over the next half century will not have such a beneficial effect. Grapes will not thrive in the warmer areas and new varieties will need to be planted.

CALIFORNIA AND THE COMING EARTHQUAKE

In 1906, the San Francisco earthquake and the subsequent fires destroyed many of the wineries in the city. Approximately 25 to 30 million gallons of wine flooded down the streets of the city from the vats of the California Wine Association. The resulting shortage of wine lasted for two years. During the fire the police were forced to soak documents in beer to preserve them from the flames.

THE CHINESE GET THE WINE HABIT

Wine is said to represent a $10 billion (£5.8 billion) market in China; about 20 per cent by value of all alcohol sold there. This is a little less than the UK percentage – and suggests a well-developed wine habit. Most of this, however, is rice wine, which is in steady decline. Though consumption of grape wine is growing at around 13 per cent per year global warming may not be enough to guarantee supplies of top-class Chinese grapes. The problem is the monsoon.

However, Western exporters are targeting the country with increasing interest, having seen the Japanese mania for top-end wines. Like the Japanese, the Chinese have a tendency to drink quality red wines on the rocks or with carbonates. Sprite and 7UP are the favourites and they contribute to the Chinese habit of *ganbei*, which – loosely translated – means 'Bottoms up' or 'Get it down your neck'. No sipping, swirling or savouring in this market; just drink it down in one – but it does help with volume sales. Whatever their drinking habits, it is likely that the Chinese will continue to embrace Western wines. Bordeaux is the favourite name, though its price is far above the 30-yuan wines (around £2) offered by the 200 or so wineries that dominate the local market.

What Colour was Homer's 'Wine-Dark Sea'?

As the habit of wine has spread, so has our perception of its colour. Five thousand years ago, Homer in the *Odyssey* makes frequent references to the 'wine-dark sea', and he appears to have regarded wine, the sea and sheep as the same colour. So, what colours did Homer see? Only four colours are mentioned in the whole of the *Iliad* and the *Odyssey*: black, white, greenish-yellow and red.

Colour is not absolute. The sense of colour is culturally linked and as language and culture evolve so too does the vocabulary of colour. All languages have a light–dark (or black-and-white) distinction. The third colour to be accorded its own 'label', according to a study in 1980 by Brent Berlin and Paul Kay, is always red. Green and yellow occupy fourth and fifth place; blue is sixth and brown seventh. In some languages – Spanish, for example – the word for 'coloured' is the same as that for 'red'.

The probability, therefore, is that Homer saw wine and the sea as 'coloured' and hence 'red'. He lacked a colour word for the 'blue' of the sea.

BOTTLE COLOURS

The colour coding of bottles evolved slowly through the eighteenth and nineteenth centuries. The original palette of colours was restricted by the cost of clear glass (driven by both tax and production costs). Most glass was 'black'. This meant dark green or brown, colours arising from the presence of metal oxides in the sand from which the glass was made. More recently, colours other than the traditional clear, green and brown have become popular.

BLUE Koala Blue – two Australian wines (Shiraz and Chardonnay) launched by (or for) Olivia Newton-John in early 2001.

BLUE POP champagne – 20 cl. cobalt-blue bottles of this Pommery champagne have been manufactured, 'designed to be drunk easily through a straw and to fit snugly in hand, allowing you to move freely and confidently around the venue in style.' The wine is sweeter and less fizzy than standard champagne. Piper-Heidsieck have a similar product – but not in a blue bottle.

PINK Not a bottle but a can. Francis Ford Coppola's 'Sofia Mini' line of sparkling wine (named after his daughter) is packaged in a 187 cl. pink can. The wine has 8 per cent Muscat in the blend to give a sweeter edge for clubbers, and is designed as a 'crossover' product. Price is $6 to $10 (£3.40 to £5.80) per single-serving can.

BLACK Not a bottle but a glass. Black glasses are often used by sommeliers in training. In a black glass it's impossible to tell whether the wine is white or red. Upmarket producer of wine glasses, Riedel, sell a black glass called the 'Blind Bind' for around £50.

RED A French wine (Vin de Pays du Jardin de la France) has a red bottle, a red plastic cork and a red label. The name, naturally, is 'Red'. The wine is white.

Champagne, in particular, has experimented with new bottle colours in its quest to conquer new markets and new occasions, though if you take at face value the reported quote of Madame Lily Bollinger you might doubt the need for such new opportunities: 'I drink it when I'm happy and when I'm sad. Sometimes I drink it when I'm alone. When I have company I consider it obligatory. I trifle with it if I'm not hungry and drink it when I am. Otherwise I never touch it – unless I'm thirsty.'

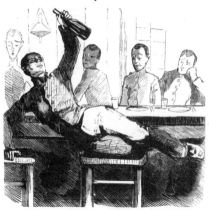

CHAMPAGNE

My only regret in life is that I did not drink more champagne.
JOHN MAYNARD KEYNES, British economist

Winston Churchill wrote the following to his brother Jack about a house he had taken for the summer: 'We live very simply here but with all the essentials well understood and provided for – hot baths, cold champagne, new peas and old brandy.'

WEIRD POP

Not exactly a champagne but similar to it was 'La Dame de Shanghai', named after the classic 1940s film *The Lady from Shanghai*, starring Rita Hayworth. The wine was the creation of Nigel Lucas, a British entrepreneur who combines soft and hard drinks with exotic herbs. La Dame de Shanghai is a *méthode traditionelle* sparkling wine from California mixed with top-quality American ginseng, which is celebrated – according to Lucas's publicity – for its qualities as 'supreme energizer, alkalizer and sensualizer'. The Millennium price was £200 a case. It is unclear whether his company, Weird Pop, survived into the new century.

THE OLDEST CHAMPAGNE

The oldest champagne drunk in recent times comes from a wooden freighter sunk by a German submarine in 1916. The *Jöngköping* was carrying 5,000 bottles of Heidsieck's Goût Américain champagne of the 1907 vintage (the same brand and year that the *Titanic* was carrying when it went down). The champagne was located 210 feet down where it had been preserved at a constant temperature of around 3° to 4°C. Bought at a Toronto auction for $4,000 (£2,300), one bottle was promptly drunk by the purchasers. They said there was still a pop on opening and a sparkle on drinking. The wine –

like much champagne of that era – was sweet rather than dry with around 42.5 grams of sugar. Today it would be described as 'rich' or 'luscious'. The colour was a deep golden yellow. It is now served by Celebrity Cruises for $7,000 (£4,000) per bottle.

A 1955 champagne, recovered by the Folkestone Diving Club from a freighter that sank in the English Channel after a collision with a Russian ship, was reported to have 'a hint of a fishy aroma and taste'.

CHAMPAGNE CAPERS

Bathing in champagne has long had an allure. The mad Queen Regina V in Erich von Stroheim's legendary unfinished silent film of 1929, *Queen Kelly*, bathes in champagne before getting down to dirtier deeds.

A persistent rumour, persistently denied, suggests that Johnny Depp once planned a champagne bath with his then girlfriend, Kate Moss. The couple were reportedly denied their frolic by an over-zealous chambermaid at London's trendy Portobello Hotel, who drained the bath (filled at an alleged cost of £750). Depp has sophisticated (and expensive) tastes. He is believed to have spent £2,600 on a single bottle of wine in a London restaurant in 2001.

Marilyn Monroe is also reported to have bathed in champagne. The 350 bottles she is said to have used would have filled the average bath to the brim.

A champagne bath was shop worker Steve Tranmer's Millennium treat to his wife of twenty years, Kim. He took advantage of a special half-price offer on Henri de Bruzier champagne at the Iceland store chain to get the bottles for £7.49, plus the benefit of an unspecified staff discount. He refused to divulge the final costs on the grounds that his wife would 'pop her cork if she knew how much I've spent'. Note: the average bath capacity is 200 litres. Assume the bath was an ungenerous half full, then Steve and Kim's bath would have cost approximately £800 – allowing for a staff discount of around 20 per cent.

A less romantic use of champagne for seduction purposes on American campuses is the administration of champagne enemas. Near-instant intoxication results – but at the risk of cramping from the bubbles and the chilly liquid ...

CHAMPAGNE LAUNCHES

The practice of breaking a bottle over the prow of a ship at the vessel's launching goes back to Viking times, when a libation of blood was used. Thousands of years earlier oxen were sacrificed.

Until the late seventeenth century, Royal Navy ships were christened by throwing a 'standing cup' (or chalice) of precious metal over the side. King William III decreed that this was too wasteful given the number of ships being built for the fast-expanding navy, and a bottle of wine was substituted. Later, champagne was used, which has remained the standard practice for all Royal Navy ships for over 300 years. In 1996, however, HMS *Sutherland* was launched with a bottle of Macallan Single Highland Malt Scotch whisky.

WHEN THE BOTTLE DOESN'T BREAK ...

Although the practice of christening ships with alcohol was the norm, it was not followed by all the commercial lines. The White Star Line, in particular, had a rather more utilitarian view of the ceremony, summarized by one Harland & Wolff shipyard worker as 'They just built 'em and shoved 'em.' This is precisely what they did for the *Titanic*, which was launched in 1911. This lack of ceremony gave rise to the legend that the *Titanic* was doomed to suffer from bad luck.

Similar stories are told about P&O's *Aurora* after the bottle failed to break first time around at the 2000 launch; the ship is said by some to be jinxed after a series of mishaps at sea. In the most recent incident, passengers who had booked for an around-the-world cruise were marooned in Southampton when the vessel suffered engine problems. The bar

was thrown open for the duration and the final total of free drinks for the passengers came to 9,200 bottles of wine and champagne as well as over 9,000 beers and 7,250 cocktails.

The Ladies Who Launch

The tradition of asking a lady to launch a vessel is generally misunderstood; they are not asked to swing the bottle themselves or throw it against the ship – unless something goes wrong, as it did for Dame Judi Dench when she came to launch *Carnival Legend* in 2002. The standard practice is to pull a rope which swings the magnum against the bow of the boat. However, this time the bottle did not break. Dame Judi then grabbed another bottle but dropped it over the side while attempting to smash it against the hull. The third bottle did smash but sprayed her with champagne in the process. Reportedly, she merely 'laughed and laughed'.

The Story of a Bubble

A bubble begins when a tiny gas pocket forms on a microscopic speck of cellulose on the surface of a wiped glass (which is why dishwashers diminish bubbles). Dissolved carbon dioxide enters the pocket, which expands and acquires buoyancy. As the bubble rises it gathers both more CO_2 and flavour molecules. When it reaches the surface it ruptures and a tiny jet of wine is released which reaches several centimetres above the surface – the tickle effect. The average bubble takes between one-hundredth and one-tenth of a second to dissipate.

They Get You Drunker, Quicker

Bubbles appear to help the alcohol reach the bloodstream faster. A study conducted at the University of Surrey in England gave matched groups of consumers equal amounts of flat and sparkling champagne. Those who consumed the bubbly had 54 milligrams of alcohol in their blood after 5 minutes. The unfortunates who drank the flat version had only 39 mg.

SMALL IS BETTER . . .

The smaller the bubble, the better the champagne. Large bubbles are the mark of lesser sparklers and are dismissed by the French as *oeils de crapaud*, or 'toad's eyes'. In a glass of champagne the bubbles of gas form at 20 microns in diameter and expand as they rise to the surface. When they reach the surface of the liquid they are approximately 1 millimetre in size, at which point they burst and release a fine spray into the air as the sides of the now empty bubble snap together under pressure from the surrounding liquid. According to scientist Bill Lembeck, the average bottle of champagne contains around 49 million bubbles. If you want more bubbles in your glass then drop in an aspirin, or scratch the bottom of the glass – both techniques are used by wine and food photographers.

. . . BUT BREAST IS NOT BEST

The above tip works equally well with the shallow coupe, the traditional (but inappropriate) champagne glass. Supposedly modelled by a porcelain maker in Sèvres from the breast of the recumbent Marie-Antoinette for her Dairy Temple at Rambouillet near Versailles, the coupe reportedly holds 160 ml., approximately the contents of a half bottle. However, it not only warms the champagne too quickly but allows all the fizz to escape almost immediately, which somewhat vitiates the point of champagne in the first place. The tall thin flute glasses are better because the smaller diameter of the surface area concentrates the aroma carried up in the bubbles. They also keep the liquid cooler.

Champagne Labels

Champagne is made from a base of dry white wine – to which sugar is added to sweeten the final liquid. This is done via the 'dosage', which is supplementary champagne used to top up the contents before corking.

Term	Meaning
Brut Sauvage, Brut Zéro, Extra Brut, Ultra Brut	No sugar in the 'dosage', though up to 6 grams per litre (g/l) of residual sugar is permissible.
Brut	Very dry, 0–15 g/l sugar.
Extra Sec	Dry, 12–20 g/l sugar.
Sec	Off dry, 17–35 g/l sugar.
Demi-sec	Sweet, 33–50 g/l sugar.
Doux	Luscious, over 50 g/l sugar.
RD (*récemment dégorgé*)	Literally, 'recently disgorged'. Means that the wine has been maturing on the lees in bottle for longer than usual. Should give greater flavour. Trademarked by Bollinger, so it's not a general description.

Wine Cocktails

Many of the great wine cocktails also have champagne as their base. Here is a selection; some with, and some without, champagne:

Name	Ingredients	Mixing
Death in the Afternoon	50 cl. Pernod Champagne	Stir Pernod in a mixing glass with ice. Pour into champagne flute and add champagne.
Madeira on the Rocks	100 cl. Madeira (not your best) 50 cl. Campari	Mix with ice.

Name	Ingredients	Mixing
Bishop	75 cl. red wine 50 cl. lemon juice 2 teaspoons of sugar syrup	Shake ingredients together with cracked ice. Add a twist of orange.
Bellini	25 cl. puréed peaches (preferably white) 125 cl. chilled champagne	Add champagne to peach purée – serve chilled.
Concorde	Cognac, champagne and pineapple juice	Shake ingredients together. Add ice.

Concorde is number nine in the top ten of hip-hop stars' cocktails. All the others in that esteemed list are brandy-based (most often Hennessy) with ingredients other than wine as the mixers.

To Open a Bottle of Champagne

Chill the wine. A bucket of cold water with a couple of dozen ice cubes added serves well. This has the side effect of reducing the interior pressure.

Strip off the foil and twist the wires to release the cage.

With your thumb on top of the cork through the mesh, twist off the cage.

Hold the cork in one hand and the bottle in the other hand, towards the base, and, if you wish, with your thumb in the punt at the bottom of the bottle.

Holding the bottle pointing away from you and others at an angle of 45°, twist the bottle gently – not the cork, which must be held firmly with the other hand.

As the cork comes away release the pressure slowly. Aim for a whisper not a pop – to preserve bubbles and wine.

Pour a small amount into a glass tilted towards you so the wine flows down the curve of the glass.

Pause, do the same with other glasses. Then return to the first and fill as required. The 'starter liquid' reduces the chance of the wine foaming over.

Note: the colder the wine, the less chance it will foam out of the bottle. Unless it has been shaken . . .

SABRETAGE

The practice of *sabretage*, or opening a champagne bottle with a cavalry sabre, does not involve a hefty swipe at the neck of the bottle. Decapitation with a sharp blade is not the aim. With the foil and wire cage removed, the champagne bottle is held pointing away from the body (and others), and with the neck raised at an angle of around 45°. The sabre is placed on the shoulder of the bottle with the blunt edge pointing up towards the neck. Using a backhand action the blade is gently but firmly slid along the neck until it hits the ridged collar – at which point the bottle top (cork and all) will fly off. The gas inside pushes away any fragments of glass.

LONGEST FLIGHT OF A CHAMPAGNE CORK

The longest recorded flight of a champagne cork is 174.5 feet at the Woodbury Vineyards in New York State on 5 June 1988. The cork was launched from 3.9 feet above ground height by Heinrich Medicus, Professor Emeritus of Physics at Rensselaer University.

CHAMPAGNE IN FLIGHT

British Airways passengers get through over a million bottles of champagne a year. Despite the post-9/11 security hysteria which saw airlines replace decent cutlery with plastic knives and forks, the 33 cl.
bottle that fuels so many business trips and economy outings has survived. This is regardless of the fact that, broken and jagged, it would make a far more terrifying weapon than the average stainless-steel fork. There was pressure from the British government to ban the bottles for that reason – resisted thus far.

In 2003, LinkPlas, a New Zealand firm, unveiled a plastic 33 cl. bottle that looks and behaves exactly like a glass bottle. They named this the 'Pettle' (as distinct from the 'pottle', which was an eighteenth-century
two-pint container). The name comes from the chemicals from which it's made, polyethylene terephthalate. It weighs just over an ounce versus the 5 ounces plus of a standard 33 cl. bottle, and, crucially, it's unbreakable. Air New Zealand is reportedly planning to roll them out on international flights in 2005 after tests on the Tasman Express. In October 2004 the Pettle won one of the 'New Zealand Plastics Industry Awards'.

Dutch airline KLM uses 46 million 25 cl. bottles of wine a year – along with 80,000 bottles of champagne and 380,000 75 cl. bottles (for those in Business and First Class).

Choosing wines for high-altitude drinking is an art in itself. Taste buds are deadened by altitude and dehydration. The average airline cabin is much drier than any desert on earth. The Sahara has around 20 per cent relative humidity, but levels on long-haul flights can go as low as 1 per cent. Stronger, sharper tastes are needed to cut through this dryness. This, claims Air New Zealand, is why un-oaked wines, with low tannin, high acidity and plentiful fruit are required. Guess what sort of wines New Zealand specializes in . . .

WINNING WINES IN THE AIR

At least one of the judges of the 2005 Cellars in the Sky awards supports this Kiwi viewpoint. Peter McCombie MW was 'disappointed' by airline wine lists and felt that too many consisted of tannic, rather closed European wines that do not show well at altitude. For him, 'the reality is that way up there, good quality New World wines probably deliver the goods more consistently.'

Altitude and dehydration are not the only factors. Tasting is best done at a pressure of around 15 pounds per square inch (psi) – though the higher the better. When you're a mile high in a plane the pressure will be around 8 psi – far lower than optimum.

There's another effect of tasting in-flight. Oxygen levels are low; recycled air not only causes drowsiness but slows down alcohol metabolization. One or two drinks on the plane is equivalent to three or four at ground level. You can experience the same effect in high cities such as Lhasa in Tibet, or Denver, Colorado.

For the record, the best Business Class cellar was that of Cathay Pacific. They won honorary mentions in several other categories – as did British Airways. The award for the best First Class selection went to Japan Airlines. They were also joint first in the category of 'Most Original' First Class list.

DECANTER'S LIST OF TOP TEN WINES

The August 2004 edition of *Decanter*, the British wine magazine, listed 100 wines 'to try before you die'. The top ten were:

Rank/Wine	Price per bottle	Comment
1. Mouton-Rothschild 1945	£3,500	'The greatest claret ever' – Michael Broadbent.
2. Château d'Yquem 1921	£1,375	'The most staggeringly rich Yquem of all time' – Broadbent again.
3. Château Latour 1961	£2,850	'May still be nearing its peak in twenty years time' – Jasper Morris MW; 100 Parker points.
4. Domaine de la Romanée-Conti, Richebourg 1959	£1,000	One of the greatest Burgundian vintages of the twentieth century – now at its zenith.
5. Domaine de la Romanée-Conti, La Tâche 1978	£1,250	'Among the greatest red Burgundies I have ever tasted' – Robert Parker.
6. Huet SA, Le Haut Lieu, Moelleux, Vouvray 1947	£400	Loire's best post-war vintage. Likely to be drinkable in 2014.
7. Penfolds Bin 60A 1962	£500	'The finest Australian wine ever made' – James Halliday. Made by Grange pioneer Max Schubert.
8. Château Pichon-Longueville Comtesse de Lalande 1982	£166	'Irresistible' – David Peppercorn MW.
9. Domaine de la Romanée-Conti, Montrachet 1978	£125	'Chardonnay at its most perfect' – Clive Coates MW.
10. Jean-Louis Chave, Cuvée Cathelin, Hermitage 1990	£75	A 'colossus: all the ingredients for another 20–30 years' – Nick Adams MW.

This top ten set would cost well over £11,000 – if you were to buy a bottle of each. In some cases you'd need to buy a dozen.

CHARDONNAY

Although Chardonnay makes it on to the top-ten list, its reputation is driven today not by Burgundy but by the Chardonnay brands that were created in Australia in the 1980s and 1990s. These somewhat sour the reputation of the grape.

To demonstrate this, here is a comment from C. P. Lin, blind New Zealand winemaker at the Mountford Estate. 'Let me tell you, Chardonnay is the prostitute of the wine industry. You can do whatever you want with it, from a dry Chablis to a heavily oaked New World wine. What you have to do is to restrict yields; that is the only way of making a better, more long-lasting Chardonnay.'

Not dissimilarly, Michael Chapoutier, seventh-generation head of Rhône producers Maison Chapoutier, described Californian Chardonnay as 'like giving Pinocchio a blowjob'.

Chardonnay's popularity rose but its reputation fell as a consequence of the Bridget Jones phenomenon. The heroine of Helen Fielding's novels mapped out her life by calories, cigarettes and glasses of wine, with Chardonnay as her tipple. Hugh Grant, who starred as the caddish Daniel Cleaver in the film versions, says, 'I live in that world – that was one of the reasons why I love the book in the first place. Half my friends are like that. We live in a world of Chardonnay and cigarettes and hopelessness.'

The ABC ('Anything But Chardonnay') movement started in the USA in the 1990s, and its name clearly spells out its manifesto. However, if there is truly no alternative to heavily wooded Chardonnay (described by critic David Marglin as 'plastic swill'), then incarcerate the wine in the freezer until it's just short of solidifying. The cooler the wine the less taste it has – a useful tip. And drink it with very salty foods.

Nor is Chardonnay necessarily exactly what it says it is. If produced in Europe, Australia, New Zealand or Hungary it must have at least 85 per cent of that variety. Not more. This means that your New Zealand Sauvignon Blanc may well have up to 15 per cent of Semillon in it. If it's produced in the USA, it will contain at least 75 per cent of the variety named on the label. Only if produced elsewhere does a single grape name on the bottle precisely define its contents.

'Chardonnay' still scores highly as a name for girls in the UK despite the cataclysmic ending of *Footballers' Wives*, the TV soap which starred Susie Amy as the beautiful but dim Chardonnay Lane-Pascoe. The template for Amy's character is popularly supposed to have been Victoria Beckham. According to Posh, she now has a second nickname: 'My hairdresser calls me Beaujolais' (or possibly Chablis). In the soap, Chardonnay died of anorexia after a spectacular career in the course of which she murdered one of her husband's teammates, and had her silicone-enhanced breasts catch fire the night before her wedding.

On the subject of footballers, 26 per cent of Britons questioned by the Wine Institute of California thought Laurent Blanc, then of Manchester United, was a grape variety.

CLARET

I can certainly see you know your wine. Most of the guests who stay here wouldn't know the difference between Bordeaux and claret.
JOHN CLEESE in *Fawlty Towers*

Mr Wint and Mr Kidd, the gay would-be killers in the 1971 film of *Diamonds Are Forever*, also get fatally confused over claret. Posing as waiters, they serve James Bond with a bottle of Mouton-Rothschild 1955 to accompany his meal. Bond, after tasting, remarks that 'for such a grand meal I had rather expected a claret.' Wint takes the bait and apologizes. 'Unfortunately, our cellars are rather poorly stocked with claret,' he replies. In the ensuing mayhem, flaming skewers of shish kebab prove to be the death of Mr Kidd.

Characters in the eighteenth- and nineteenth-century novels by writers such as Sir Walter Scott and William Thackeray are frequently found calling for 'bumpers of claret' that they then 'tossed off'. The use of 'bumper' in this sense – in which the liquid is described as 'bumping' against the rim, or overflowing – now survives in common usage only in the phrase 'a bumper harvest'. It was far more commonly used two hundred years ago for an abundance of any commodity, but the term is believed to derive from full glasses of beer and wine.

PUSH THE BOAT OUT

Lord Nelson, hero of Trafalgar, lost his arm in battle in 1797. To ensure that he could still circulate drinks effectively when entertaining his captains he commissioned a small model of a ship, with wheels, to be made from sterling silver. This held two decanters of wine and could be pushed around the Admiral's table with ease.

THE FIRST BRAND NAME IN WINE

Earlier still, Samuel Pepys extolled the virtues of one particular claret (the only one he refers to by name). His diary note for 10 April 1663 describes how he made his way ' . . . to the Royall Oake Taverne in Lombard-street [. . .] And here drunk a sort of French wine called Ho Bryan, that hath a good and most perticular taste that I never met with.' It was of course Château Haut-Brion, one of the original first growths in the 1855 classification. In London in the seventeenth century, Haut-Brion (or Pontac, as it was also

known) fetched 7 shillings a bottle, 3.5 times the price of Spanish wine. Given that £1 then was worth about £90 today, the cost of the wine in today's money was around £30. The place to drink it was a restaurant called The Pontac's Head, named by and for François-Auguste de Pontac, a wine entrepreneur whose business flourished in London from 1666 onwards. Selling the products of his father's estate, Pontac, in the words of one wine writer, turned Haut-Brion into the world's first cult wine. It was the first wine to be referred to by the name of the château rather than the generic 'claret' or 'clairet' – references to which are sprinkled through Pepys's diary.

Pepys also drank Spanish red wine and had a 'runlet' of Tent in his cellar. A runlet was a small cask, and Tent was the anglicization of *tintilla* or *tinta di Rota*, the finest red wine of Andalusia. The name survived until the nineteenth century and Hugh Johnson has proposed its reintroduction as a generic term for dark red wines.

CLARET AND STRAWBERRIES

An urban myth of the nineteenth century appears to have held that a strawberry in a glass of claret tempered the 'heating' effect of the wine. A City alderman, having drunk deep, blamed his hangover not on the six bottles of claret that he had imbibed but on 'that confounded single strawberry' that he had kept all night in the bottom of his glass.

Strawberry Soup with Claret

Take 500 grams of strawberries and cook until the fruit is soft. Purée the fruit in a blender and mix the purée with an equal amount of claret (or claret and water mixed to taste). Strain (if preferred) and then chill. Serve with unsweetened whipped cream or with cream flavoured with sugar and vanilla. Sprinkle with nutmeg before serving. The soup is better tart than sweet.

Claret and Confusion

The rivalry between Burgundy and Bordeaux has endured for hundreds of years. Anthelme Brillat-Savarin, the greatest of all French gourmands, was once asked by a lady of his acquaintance for his preference. Was it Burgundy or Bordeaux? His answer? 'That, madame, is a question I take so much pleasure in investigating that I postpone from week to week the pronouncement of a verdict.' Harry Waugh, doyen of English wine writers in the 1950s, was asked (the gender of *his* interrogator is unknown) when he had last confused Burgundy and Bordeaux. 'Not since lunchtime,' was his succinct and sensible response.

Burgundy – Duty and Domesticity

The First Duty of wine is to be red . . . the second is to be a Burgundy.
Harry Waugh, English wine writer

The pretensions of wine snobs were mocked by James Thurber in the caption to one of his most famous *New Yorker* cartoons. As the host opens a bottle he announces to his guests, 'It's only a naive domestic Burgundy without any breeding but I think you'll be amused by its presumption.'

JESUS JUICE

Burgundy of course is made from the Pinot Noir grape. Pinot Noir is supposedly the favourite grape of troubled singer Michael Jackson. He is alleged to swig it from soft-drink cans so that his drinking habits cannot be easily detected. White wine is reputedly called 'Jesus Juice' and red wine 'Jesus Blood' by Jackson, though the former appears to be used as a generic title by Jackson commentators.

THE PHEROMONES OF PINOT

Lovers of Pinot Noir – also a grape from which champagne is made – talk of 'fine perfumed wine with sex appeal' (Robert Joseph), the 'peacock's tail flare on the finish' (James Halliday) and the ability of the greatest Burgundies to 'blossom flowers' (Michael Bettane). Gina Gallo, winemaker for the Gallo Sonoma brand, says that 'when you fall in love with wine, you end up loving Pinot Noir.' She has planted 600 acres of Pinot Noir to prove her point.

Canadian writer Konrad Ejbich has no doubts about Pinot's sexiness. He claims to look for places where he 'can drink it with one hand under the table' and describes it as 'heaven in a glass . . . the colour of ruby lips. It smells like great sex and tastes like the ripest strawberries, raspberries and black cherries all at once.'

Some research has suggested that the pheromones of the Pinot Noir grape are closely akin to male pheromones – musky, slightly feral, somewhat earthy. The female pheromones (typified by fish and milky cheese) are harder to find in wine, though Australian winemaker Max Lake has suggested that champagne contains isovaleric acid, which gives off the smell of soft cheese.

Possibly a Californian blurb-writer had Pinot's reputation for sexiness in mind when he wrote the following back-label copy for Armida 1999 Russian Valley Pinot Noir. 'Remember the last time you walked through a Moroccan brothel? As your eyes adjusted from sunlight to un-light, the aroma of cinnamon and clove, of curry and ginger moved through the air like a blown kiss . . . Can't afford a trip back to Morocco? The 1999 Pinot Noir is the next best thing to being there.'

RIESLING

Riesling is the grape that wine writers and wine experts tend to nominate as their favourite white grape. The great wine-drinking public – often depicted as hopelessly in thrall to the dubious charms of Chardonnay – appear neither to know about nor to care for Riesling's blend of steely acidity, intense cool aroma and subtle, citrus fruit. It's their loss and the insider's gain, since great Riesling is still dramatically underpriced.

Part of the problem is that Rhine Riesling (the true Riesling of Germany, Austria and Australia) has what some would see as a malign younger brother, which goes under the name of Welschriesling or Laski Riesling.

In the right hands, this lesser Riesling is used to create superlative late-harvest wines in Austria and elsewhere, but as an everyday drinking wine it is rarely better than fresh and fruity.

Good (white Riesling)	*Not so good (except in dessert wines)*
Rhine Riesling (South Africa)	Riesling Italico (Italy)
Weisser Riesling	Welschriesling (Austria)
Riesling Renano (Italy)	Rizling (anywhere)
White Riesling	Olasz Riesling (Hungary)
Johannisberg Riesling (USA)	Laski Riesling (Slovenia, Croatia)
Renski Rizling (Slovenia)	Rizling Vlassky (Slovakia)

American wine writer Robin Garr suggests Riesling marketers may be missing a trick. 'I have never fully understood why German Riesling isn't a runaway bestseller, particularly in the US, where many people drink sweet soft drinks by the tank-car load. Riesling [is] light, fresh, low in calories, easy to quaff and slightly sweet, with fresh-fruit sugar nicely balanced by refreshing acidity. You could call it a soft drink for adults!'

The irony is that Hock (from the town of Hochheimer) was one of the world's most expensive wines in the eighteenth and nineteenth centuries. At the Christie's sale of 1808 a dozen bottles of 'Very Old Hock' sold for over £10. This, according to Michael Broadbent, was the highest price for any wine at auction between 1766 and the 1880s. Hock was Queen Victoria's favourite and her preference undoubtedly influenced tastes in the second half of the nineteenth century.

Even a 1912 wine list (cited in Thomas Burke's 1934 memoir of London, *City of Encounters*), shows Lafite 1890 at 40 shillings (£2) a dozen compared to Bernkastler Doktor of 1907 at 63 shillings (£3.15) a dozen.

WOMEN AND WINE

Jancis Robinson's status as 'HRH of the British wine scene' is not just down to her vivid personality, her erudition and her industry. There is good evidence that women are biologically better tasters.

MOST VALUABLE NOSE

The nose (and taste buds) of Angela Mount, senior wine buyer for British supermarket chain Somerfield, is insured for £10 million. The policy forbids her from smoking. It has also been reported that Tesco has evidence to suggest that pregnant women make the best tasters since they have the most sensitive noses.

WOMEN SMELL BETTER

Research in the USA using FMRI technology (otherwise known as Functional Magnetic Resonance Imaging) appears to prove conclusively that the 25 per cent of people who are 'super-tasters' (those with a particularly high sensitivity to aromas and taste) are twice as likely to be female as male. Women in their reproductive years are significantly more sensitive than all other groups – male and female. This is thought to be linked to the evolutionary advantage of being able to identify toxins in foods. Other evidence suggests that women simply use their brain more intensively when tasting – FMRI scans show up to eight times greater usage.

Women are also more likely to be able to improve their sense of smell with practice, although this ability is not confined to the female gender. The receptors in the nose are replaced more frequently than cells in almost any other part of the body, and those that are replaced are those we use most. In other words, we can re-grow our 'nose' to suit our favourite smells, and to recognize them better in the future.

Jacques Lardière, technical director of Maison Louis Jadot, claims that women swill wine in the opposite direction to men. That may affect the aromas – if it's true.

WHICH WINE WOULD YOU WEAR?

Another female perspective on wine comes from Leslie Sbrocco, American author of *Wine For Women: A Guide to Buying, Pairing and Sharing Wine*, who represents wine as clothing. Here are her comparisons.

Wine type	Clothing analogy
Sauvignon Blanc	Crisp white blouse or freshly laundered cotton shirt
Merlot	Soft, silky cashmere sweater
Syrah	Stylish red leather bag
Cabernet Sauvignon	A knock-out business suit
Riesling	A comfortable (but figure-enhancing) bra
Chardonnay	Basic black
Sangiovese	Chic Italian high heels
Pinot Noir	Elegant, classy and glamorous – the silk dress of reds
Zinfandel	Black leather trousers that add an element of untamed intrigue to your wardrobe

Sara Gagnon, winemaker at Olympic Cellars, explicitly targets some of her wines at women. The label for Working Girl White suggests that it's 'a sassy no-nonsense blend of Chardonnay and Riesling that will ease the crankiness and stress of a long, sweltering day in pantyhose and pumps.' On the other hand, Rosé the Riveter 'just rocks' with its blend of redcurrant and raspberry aromas and pomegranate and cranberry flavours. Just in case you're wondering, these wines are also multiple-award winners in the winemaking areas of north-west USA. The set of Working Girl wines is completed by Go Girl Red, a 'lush little number' blended from Merlot and Lemberger.

WINE AND BALSAMIC VINEGAR

Wine vinegar is made from wine. Balsamic vinegar is not. The best wine vinegar is produced by the Orléans method, which entails ageing the vinegar in wood (just like the best wine). Balsamic vinegar (for which the first literary reference dates back to 1046, when a barrel was given to the Holy Roman Emperor Henry III) was originally made with wine vinegar. Since 1861, however, true balsamic vinegar has been made from the fresh (that is, unfermented) juice of white grapes with a high sugar content (often Trebbiano). The just-fermenting must is evaporated in a copper kettle and then aged (and further evaporated) in barrels of oak, ash and cherrywood. At 10-per-cent evaporation per year within the container, 100 litres will become 15 litres after a dozen years. Commercial-grade balsamic vinegar is red-wine vinegar mixed with fresh must and caramel to add colour.

WINE AND CHOCOLATE

Many purists will flatly deny that any acceptable match can be made. Certainly, the intense sweetness of chocolate and its ability to carpet-bomb the taste buds makes matching wine with the sweet a tricky proposition, and the sweeter the chocolate the harder this becomes.

There are no simple rules but writers with more imagination, and perhaps greater knowledge, have numerous suggestions.

Sweet sparkling wines such as Asti Spumante work well with chocolate desserts. Wines made from Muscat grapes (like Asti) tend to have the required aromatic intensity and sweetness. Try Muscat de Beaumes de Venise with chocolate meringue. Fortified white and red wines work well. Vin Jaune, the fabled 'yellow wine' from the Jura region of France, has the concentration to deal with many chocolate dishes and a local chocolatier, M. Hirsinger, has developed a range of chocolates to eat with the Jura wines. Banyuls – made in the South of France from Grenache grapes – has both the weight and the sweetness to take chocolate on. Recioto, a sweet red wine made from dried grapes in Northern Italy, has a similar power, even though it is not fortified. Sherries made from the Pedro Ximénez grape work wonders. Try the excellent Gonzalez Byass range.

The more bitter the chocolate the easier it is to match. If the chocolate is used for savoury sauces then the choice can be widened to powerful, dry red wines such as Zinfandel or Merlot – particularly when these have chocolatey notes. Top wines from the Chianti region, such as Castello di Bossi's fabled single-vineyard Girolamo, also prove surprisingly good partners. A certain touch of bitterness, an earthy quality and the roasted notes of powerful, warm-climate reds match the characteristics of the bitter chocolate itself.

For those who want to conduct controlled experiments, the San Francisco Chocolate Factory sells a 'Wine Lovers' Chocolate Collection'. Each of their three tins contains chocolate drops of increasingly higher levels of cocoa solids (and hence bitterness) and comes with recommendations for signature wines. Their selections include Zinfandel for the highest level of cocoa solids and port for the lightest. Many – though not all – would disagree with that latter recommendation.

Wine and Food – Matches and Mismatches

'Red wine with meat, white wine with fish,' goes the age-old maxim. Wrong – or at least, no more than half right. Red wine with heavy tannins works well with steak because the tannins combine with the proteins in the meat and soften both the wine and the steak.

However, some lighter red wines work perfectly with fish – notably Cabernet Franc and many Italian wines. Lighter reds can also work with Thai food, though sweeter, spicier whites are usually better. Alexander de Lur-Saluces of Yquem maintains Sauternes can be drunk throughout such a meal.

Michael Broadbent, as so often, has safe advice: 'Decide which is the soloist and which the accompanist.' Heavy sauces and complex dishes are not the best accompaniment to great wine. Simplicity is all.

Matching Wine's Worst Enemies

Four notoriously tricky foods to match with wine are asparagus, globe artichokes, tomatoes and eggs.

Asparagus is tricky because its intense grassy flavour and acidic sulphurous components make most wine taste odd. Words like 'vegetal', 'dank' and 'over-oaked' all come up. One solution is to grill the asparagus to sweeten the flavour. Then serve with a wine with

high acid but good levels of fruit – for example New Zealand Sauvignon Blanc. Avoid oaked Chardonnays or any wines with high tannin. Pinot Noir works well with grilled asparagus.

Artichokes are equally tricky. Cynarin, which dominates their flavour profile, makes wines taste sweet. Hence one answer is to serve them with bone-dry wines – French Sauvignon Blanc, the driest of Vouvrays or champagne brut. Another answer is to use sauces to take the edge off the bitterness and then match the wine to the sauce.

Tomatoes are only a challenge because of their high acidity. Go for high-acid wines, red or white, and the problems are diminished. Provençal rosé will often work well – indicating that the old adage of pairing food with wines of that region is always a useful strategy if all else fails.

Eggs appear to flatten wine. An omelette on its own is a serious challenge to the wine matcher. Best to add an ingredient to the eggs – meat, crab, vegetables – and match to the ingredient. If you must find a match for the eggs, then go for intensely flavoured white wines. Again, avoid tannic wines.

THE MAP OF THE TONGUE

Until recently it was believed that four basic tastes were detectable by the human palate – whether wine or food was at issue. These were sweetness, bitterness, sourness (or acidity) and saltiness. Classic wine education asserts confidently that these can be mapped to different locations on the tongue, with sweetness on the tip, saltiness on either side just back from the tip, sour tastes on the edge but even further back, and bitterness at the back of the tongue in the centre. This basic diagram goes back over a hundred years but it turns out that it is inaccurate in several ways.

Firstly, there is a fifth taste – *unami*, or savoury. This is the taste of soy sauce.

Secondly, more recent evidence suggests that while there are variations in detection thresholds at different sites on the tongue these are small and, apart from the bitter taste which is more easily detected at the back of the tongue, are of no practical value for tasting purposes. What *is* important, however, is the number of taste receptors (which can vary hugely between individuals) and the distribution of those taste receptors. An average number is around 7,000.

Thirdly, the amount of saliva produced varies greatly by individual and this too affects our perceptions of taste.

ROBOTONGUE

If your palate isn't up to it then there is the Robotongue. Developed in Brazil and Wales it has the ability to detect flavours at levels far lower than the human palate can achieve, with the further advantage that – unlike the human palate – it does not get tired and does not suffer from colds and flu. Magnetic Resonance Imaging (MRI) can also be used to detect traces of acetic acid in wine – but not the TCA bacteria that cause cork taint.

I, WINEMAKER

Another technological intervention into winemaking is the mechanization of grape-treading. For centuries, human feet have been used to pound grapes. Port, in particular, has traditionally used chains of treaders, arms around each others' waists for stability, to crush grapes in the granite troughs or *lagares*. Biomechanically speaking, feet have many advantages. They exert gentle pressure and friction that helps to break down the grape skins and liberate colour and tannin, they do not crush grape pips (which would increase tannin levels in the wine), and they help with micro-oxygenation of the must by raising the skins from the floor of the *lagar* as they lift.

However, the process is not very hygienic and the temperature of feet (around 37°C) tends to reduce the fruit in the resultant wine. The solution was obvious – robotic feet. They do not get tired; they do not get drunk; they do not fall over or fight with their neighbours. The Symington family, which controls port brands such as Dow's, Warre's, Graham's and Quinta do Vesuvio, have now created such feet.

The silicon-coated feet exert 120 grams per cm², the same as the average human foot; they can be programmed to tread more softly in the later stages to prevent over-extraction from the skins, and they are rectangular in shape to encourage a film of must to stick to them as they rise.

I, WINE WAITER

It is said that in the 1980s an Edinburgh restaurant installed a robot (named Donic) to act as its wine waiter. He was ill-behaved (and presumably ill-programmed), pouring wine on the carpet and smashing furniture. The manufacturers blamed the restaurant's DJ, who had been in charge of setting up Donic's systems.

'Good Wine Needs No Bush'

This Shakespeare quotation (from the epilogue to *As You Like It*) has ancient roots. The Roman writer of mimes, Publilius Syrus, noted in the first century BC that 'you need not hang up the ivy branch over the wine that will sell.' (*Sentences*, No. 968). The Emperor Charlemagne – perhaps informed by his reading of the classics – gave winegrowers the right to sell direct to customers and to use a green branch outside their establishment to advertise this facility. This right was confirmed by succeeding Holy Roman Emperors, and Viennese growers maintain this tradition in the *Heurigen*; Austrian drinking establishments that surround the city and offer wine and food to passers-by.

Selling Wine – The Ann Summers and Avon Styles

Tupperware has now largely folded its tents and stolen away but Avon and Ann Summers, in their different ways, both show that network selling can be a financial hit. Stockbroker Nigel Johnson-Hill and his wife originally created a mail-order wine company specializing in French wines in the 1980s. The Vintry – named after the old name for a wine store and the City of London ward where Chaucer was born – acquired its first network-sales capacity in 1990 when another family joined. There are now thirteen vintrys operating around the UK. Most of them are in the south-west of Britain, and many of the salespeople are farmers. Each vintry (with a small 'v' to distinguish it from the parent company) takes 10-per-cent commission on the wine it sells from the company's extensive list of French wines, which is now augmented by some Australian and South African selections. The local vintrys each turn over between £50,000 and £100,000 a year and the company is eager to expand its range.

BEAUJOLAIS NOUVEAU – THE GREAT WINE RACE

The most successful promotional idea ever conceived for wine is that of Beaujolais Nouveau. Beaujolais Primeur (its proper term, since it's a wine released before the spring immediately after the harvest) has always been drunk with gusto in the bars of Lyons and as soon after vinification as possible. The trade (and its boozy consequences) was regulated in 1938, but in 1951 the rules were revoked and an official mid-November release date was set for what was then officially called Beaujolais Nouveau.

The wine is made from hand-harvested Gamay *noir à jus blanc* grapes, and vinified via carbonic maceration or whole-berry fermentation which gives the wine, at its best, a vibrant, fresh and fruity character with low tannins. If it's badly made, or suffers a poor year, it can taste like raspberry jam. Whatever the quality on release, it will not improve. It's a wine made for drinking lightly chilled, for drinking young and for drinking in gulps rather than delicate sips.

After a number of minor changes the release date has become the third Thursday of November – traditionally at one minute past midnight. The first 'race' was in the 1950s when British wine merchants used to load their lorries and set off for Calais at the stroke of midnight. Allan Hall, then wine correspondent of the *Sunday Times*, offered to exchange the first bottle of Beaujolais Nouveau to hit his desk for a bottle of champagne. The tradition gathered force and  more and more elaborate techniques evolved for getting the wine back to the UK as close as possible to that one-minute-past-midnight deadline. Military jets, vintage cars and fast motorbikes were all conscripted. In other parts of the world, elephants, rickshaws and runners have played their part.

The race has now lost its cachet – certainly in the UK – and the regulations have changed to allow for the wine to be distributed to its final destination in time for release at the appointed time. Japan now takes the lion's share with over 800,000 cases in 2004. Of these, 80 per cent were reportedly drunk at home. The next highest consumers are the Americans, but distribution stretches as far as Korea, Vietnam and Australia. In the USA, impatient fans can buy 'air nouveau' at around $10 (£5.80) a bottle or wait a month and pick up 'boat nouveau' for $2 less. Typically, the higher the price, the higher the consumption. Where the price has slumped, as in the UK, consumption has fallen away dramatically.

Sales are now over 70 million bottles a year – up from around a million forty-five years ago. Georges Duboeuf, the inspiration behind the modern Beaujolais Nouveau phenomenon, is responsible for some 4 million of those. It's been derided as 'Kool-Aid wine', but it's been a great commercial success, even if that success has been bought at the expense of Beaujolais's more serious side and its finer wines.

However, the Beaujolais producers retained enough clout to win a judgement in 2003 against *Lyon Mag*, which quoted the comments of Belgian François Mausse of the Grand Jury of European Wine Tasters, who said the wine was a *vin de merde* or, slightly more politely, 'lightly fermented alcoholized fruit juice'. *Lyon Mag* was fined €300,000 (£210,000).

THE REAL WINE RACE –
THE MARATHON DU MÉDOC

The greatest marathon of the wine world is undoubtedly the Marathon du Médoc, which is run annually between fifty-nine Bordeaux châteaux. It is billed as the 'Longest Marathon in the World', and there are eighteen wine stops. In the last few miles

more enticing treats such as oysters, steak and cheese are on offer. The stops include Château Lafite-Rothschild, Château Gruaud-Larose and Château Puy-Lacoste. The winner wins his weight in Grand Cru wine – but it is unlikely that he (or she) will have had much time to sample the good things on offer during the race. Dedicated runners sample everything and still finish in under three hours. The remainder of the 8,000 or so starters take their time, sample the produce on offer and hope to finish inside the regulation six hours and fifteen minutes. Each year a medical symposium discusses running-related injuries. The 2001 topic was 'Intoxication from Absorption of Water'. There are also wine marathons in the Lubéron and Beaujolais.

THE FULL MONTY – WINE STYLE

Five of the 2005 runners in the Marathon du Médoc also took part in the UK wine trade's first 'Full Monty'. On behalf of the Prostate Cancer Charity, two of the UK's Masters of Wine, Michael Palij and Tim Atkin, joined five colleagues in displaying their all at a women-only charity event.

JAMES BOND'S WINE

The mass media can play a major part in driving wine sales. Ian Fleming's taste in wine has been described as 'vulgar' but Tom Stevenson, the foremost writer on champagne in the English language, has credited Fleming with inspiring in English drinkers the taste for *blanc de blancs* champagne. *Blanc de blancs* is now defined as champagne made from 100 per cent Chardonnay, but when Fleming was writing it could include any or all of the white grapes allowed in champagne, including such relative rarities as Petit Meslier and Arbanne.

James Bond has, of course, become famous for the vodka martini ('shaken not stirred') but wine – particularly champagne – is at least as important as the hard stuff.

Everyday wines get a mention every now and then. For instance, when he is despatched to Shrublands, the health spa, his reveries centre around revenge against Count Lippe (*Thunderball*'s villain), his beautiful nurse, Patricia, and food. In particular he has 'a passionate longing for a large dish of spaghetti bolognese containing plenty of chopped garlic and accompanied by a whole bottle of the cheapest, rawest Chianti.' He gets his way – and Nurse Patricia – in Brighton.

In *From Russia with Love*, Bond misses a Chianti clue. Red Grant, the KGB assassin, orders Chianti with his fish course while dining on the Orient Express. When, at first, Bond is overpowered by Grant, he remarks, 'Red wine with fish. That should have told me something.' Unlike every other book (and film) featuring Bond, champagne does not make an appearance.

BOND'S WINES – BY THE BOOK

From Russia with Love

Calvet Bordeaux	Enjoyed on the train.
Chianti Broglio	Shared with Tatiana on the train back from Istanbul.
Kavakladere	'Rich, coarse Burgundy' wine from Turkey's oldest private-sector winemaker.

Casino Royale

Taittinger Brut Blanc de Blancs 1943	'The finest champagne in the world' – an anonymous gift in the casino.
Veuve Clicquot champagne	Enjoyed with Vesper Lynd in the casino nightclub after his defeat of Le Chiffre at baccarat.

Diamonds are Forever

Clicquot Rosé	'A faint hint of strawberries' – champagne drunk with Tiffany Case at the 21 Club in New York.
Bollinger (quarter bottle)	Sent by Tiffany to his cabin on the *Queen Elizabeth* – along with sauce Béarnaise she has made to accompany steak canapés.

Moonraker

Dom Pérignon 1946	Wine waiter's suggestion at Blades, M.'s club. Bond adds Benzedrine before his card game with Hugo Drax – and a further bottle of champagne.

Goldfinger

Pommery pink champagne	Drunk from 1-pint silver tankards with stone crabs at Bill's on the Beach in Miami.
Piesporter Goldtröpfchen	Recommended by and drunk with Auric Goldfinger (naturally).
Mouton-Rothschild 1947	The same dinner – drunk with roast duckling.
Rosé d'Anjou	Well-iced with dinner at the Hôtel du Gare in Orléans.
Mâcon	Part of the picnic with Tilly Masterton – along with sausage, bread and butter.
Fendant	Bond has a carafe of this Swiss white for dinner in Geneva.

Thunderball

Chianti	Imbibed in Brighton to accompany his garlic-laden spaghetti bolognese.
Clicquot Rosé	Drunk with Beluga caviar in the casino at Nassau with Domino.

On Her Majesty's Secret Service

Taittinger Blanc de Blancs	Consumed 'rather fast' in his hotel room in Royale-les-Eaux.
Mouton-Rothschild 1953	Half-bottle to accompany his 'best ever' roast partridge before joining the play in the casino.
Krug champagne	Half-bottle drunk in the casino bar – just before La Comtesse Teresa di Vicenzo (also known as Tracy) introduces herself.
Riquewihr	Alsatian white wine compared by Draco to cat's pee – but acceptable when drunk with 'good Strasbourg sausage' at Draco's château.

Bond's enduring passion is for champagne – especially pink champagne. In the books his favourite is Taittinger, while in the films it's Bollinger – 'the official champagne'. Bond (in the person of Timothy Dalton) regards Bollinger RD as his favourite.

A set of nineteen magnums etched with themes from the Bond films sold for $360,000 (£250,000) at the Napa Valley Wine Auctions in 1997.

A New Zealand winery, Spy Valley, is located close to a secret US monitoring base in Marlborough. Blair Gibbs, general manager of the winery, which specializes in Riesling, Gewürztraminer, Pinot Noir, Chardonnay and Sauvignon Blanc, is planning to release the wine as 'Spy Valley, 007'. The American spies are apparently good customers of the company.

REALITY TV – *BIG BROTHER* AND BLACK TOWER

The 2002 UK series of *Big Brother* provided a major plug for the 1970s favourite of British drinkers – Black Tower. Black Tower is a medium-sweet German wine from the Rheinhessen out of the Blue

Nun school of winemaking. The winner of the 2002 series, Kate Lawler, now has a lifetime's supply donated by the grateful distributor, Matthew Clark. She insisted on putting it on the weekly shopping list – even downgrading the quality of the champagne to buy more wine. The result was a 40-per-cent increase in sales over a nine-week period.

Alcohol is integral to *Big Brother* around the world (except the teen versions), but only in the UK can you hire out the *Big Brother* house for corporate events. These come with your choice of beer, wine or vintage champagne (for a fee). The top package costs £30,000 per night and includes filming of the entire event. The house will hold one hundred people for a party or eighty people for a dinner party.

WINE IN THE SOAPS

Nigel Pargetter in BBC Radio 4's *The Archers* went through a spell of enthusiasm for making English sparkling wine in 2003 but this has now waned – possibly because of the climatic difficulties of growing champagne-style grapes just south of Birmingham.

In *Coronation Street*, when the actors drink wine in the Rover's Return they are not getting much alcohol. White wine is water with added lime juice, red wine is Vimto (or blackcurrant juice), vodka is just pure water and dark spirits such as whisky or brandy are made from burnt sugar and water. This practice would go down badly with Len Evans, the great Australian wineman.

The 'Theory of Consumption'

The theory of consumption – as credited to Len Evans, Australian bon viveur – goes as follows. He drinks a bottle of wine a day. Given another twenty years to live, he has around 7,300 bottles to go. It follows that none of these must be wasted. Therefore, every bottle must give pleasure and stimulate interest. Another theory of consumption suggests that the ideal conclusion to one's life is to die with just a handful of bottles left in the cellar. These – if you are generous – are for the executors. André Simon, one of the greatest connoisseurs of wine in the twentieth century, and founder of the International Wine and Food Society, believed that 'a man dies too young if he leaves any wine in his cellar.' He almost made it. When he died at the age of ninety-three just two magnums of claret remained in his personal cellar.

The 'Theory of Consumption' in Practice – The Single Bottle Club

Len Evans has many claims to fame. Born in England, he emigrated to Australia in 1955 and, working for the Hilton hotel chain, became immersed in wine. His work for the Australian Wine Board in the 1960s persuaded Australians that real men could and should drink table wine. He told the story of how he once asked for wine in a country hotel. The bartender looked at him through narrowed eyes before asking, 'What are you, some kind of poof?'

Evans laid the foundation for the modern Australian wine industry. He invented the Wine Options game (see page 171) which helped turn blind tasting into a competitive sport. He was also the founder of the Single Bottle Club in 1977.

This may sound a little puritanical. It is not. The 'single bottle' of the club title may be shared between many but, on the other hand, there are many single bottles. The sixteenth dinner, held at Len Evans's estate in 1992, featured twelve vintages of Château Latour and six vintages of Yquem going back to 1912.

This is a club dedicated to consuming rather than preserving bottles of rare wine. The first dinner – held in honour of Michael Broadbent – featured a bottle of 1727 Rüdesheimer Apostelwein.

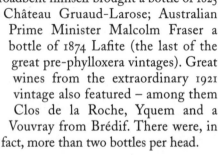

Broadbent himself brought a bottle of 1825 Château Gruaud-Larose; Australian Prime Minister Malcolm Fraser a bottle of 1874 Lafite (the last of the great pre-phylloxera vintages). Great wines from the extraordinary 1921 vintage also featured – among them Clos de la Roche, Yquem and a Vouvray from Brédif. There were, in fact, more than two bottles per head.

The oldest wine the club has ever tasted is the 1646 Tokay, which is featured earlier in this book.

The Wine Options Game

Len Evans's Wine Options game can be played by all levels from professional tasters to enthusiastic amateurs. The essence of the game – for there are strict rules available – is that the Question Master asks a series of questions about a wine that all participants have tasted. It begins with an easy question – such as, 'Is this wine Old World or New World?' – and proceeds by degrees to the toughest. You can either mark each question and allow participants to continue until the end or, more properly, knock out those who fail each round. In this disciplined version of the game, the winner is the last person standing.

If you are running the game it is your responsibility to prepare the questions and your duty to have a tie-breaker ready if more than one person gets to the end of your sequence unchallenged.

'Call My Wine Bluff'

Another useful game for large gatherings is 'Call My Wine Bluff'. A wine is tasted by the assembled participants. Each person in a

group of panellists reads out their personal tasting note and purported attribution of the wine. The task of the audience is to work out which of the notes and attributions is correct. This game is limited only by the imagination and verbal prowess of the panellists. It well reveals the limitations of most people's taste buds.

THE 'SIDEWAYS GAME'

This game has a lighter touch – though it may be equally revealing. The dinner-party question is simple: 'If you were a grape, what grape would you be?' The supplementary is 'and why?' It is surprisingly effective as an ice-breaker.

MOST FRUSTRATING WINE GIFT

The leading candidate is the 'Don't Break the Bottle' wooden wine puzzle. Three pieces of wood linked by a rope with a ball on the end enclose the bottle. To get the wine out you have to manipulate the puzzle. Hours of fun – and frustration – all yours, for around £15.

Index

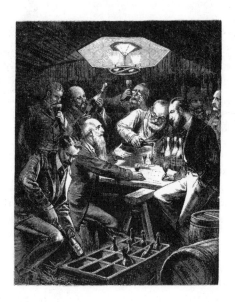

Index